STARTING YOUR OWN PRACTICE

STARTING YOUR OWN PRACTICE

THE INDEPENDENCE GUIDE FOR PROFESSIONAL SERVICE PROVIDERS

ROBERT FRAGASSO

WILEY

John Wiley & Sons, Inc.

For general information on our other products and services, please contact our Customer Care Department within the United States at 800-762-2974, outside the United States at 317-572-3993 or fax 317-572-4002.

Wiley also publishes its books in a variety of electronic formats. Some content that appears in print may not be available in electronic books. For more information about Wiley products, visit our web site at www.wiley.com.

Library of Congress Cataloging-in-Publication Data:

Fragasso, Robert, 1945–

    Starting your own practice : the independence guide for professional service providers / Robert Fragasso.

      p. cm.

ISBN-13 978-0-471-73305-8 (cloth)

ISBN-10 0-471-73305-9 (cloth)

    1. Financial planners.   2. Investment advisors.   3. New business enterprises—Planning. I. Title

HG179.5.F73 2005

332.6'068'1—dc   2005004694

Printed in the United States of America

10 9 8 7 6 5 4 3 2 1

To my children, Christine, Kathleen, and Vicki; their husbands, Brian and Mike; and my grandchildren, Kaitlyn, Bailey, and Connor, who provide the reason to continually improve our business and also to my business associates and clients who make it fun.

CONTENTS

FOREWORD

In the last two decades, we have witnessed a dramatic shift in the U.S. economy, moving from a manufacturing-based economy to a service-based economy. Over the next 20 years, I believe the economic evolution will be even more dramatic as employees realize the flexibility a service-based economy can provide to them. Maybe one of the single greatest shifts in the history of our economy is yet to come as more and more workers in this service-based economy cut the ties to their employers and go into business for themselves. If you want to be a part of this new wave, your first step is to read *Starting Your Own Practice: The Independence Guide for Professional Service Providers.* This book begins by helping you decide if you should go into business for yourself. Then it gives you a logical, easy to read, step-by-step game plan of how to make it happen. It's a no-nonsense look at what it takes—spending equal time addressing what's good about being in business for yourself as well as what's bad about it.

It is destined to be one of the best business "how-to" books ever written. This book will become your blueprint for success if you decide to go down the path of going into business for yourself.

Starting Your Own Practice: The Independence Guide for Professional Service Providers is written through the eyes of an investment advisor entrepreneur. Not just any investment advisor, but one of the very best anywhere. I ought to know; I travel the world meeting with tens of thousands of financial advisors each year, and Robert Fragasso is at the top of that list. He is not just a great investment advisor, he is a savvy and astute businessman with the strong moral and ethical fiber this country needs. We all can learn from his advice.

This book, however, is not just about investment advisors, it's about anyone in the service economy, insurance agents, real estate professionals, attorneys, accountants, and so on, who want to become independent and run their own business. The principles for success are the same regardless of what part of the service economy you find yourself in. It's somewhat ironic to me that the author of this book would be from Pittsburgh, the city that best represents how to move from the manufacturing to service economy. So now it is only fitting that a fellow Pittsburgher will help us with this final economic shift of moving to the top of the service economy by going into business for yourself.

Starting Your Own Practice: The Independence Guide for Professional Service Providers *can change your life if you give it a chance.*

—Dr. Bob Froehlich,
Chairman Investor Strategy Committee,
Scudder Investments

PREFACE

This book will help you decide if you wish to go into business for yourself. And it will help you plan your move and structure the marketing, managing, staffing, and general operation of your business. The book is written primarily for service providers wishing to move to independence, including investment advisors and brokers, insurance agents, real estate professionals, architects, attorneys, accountants, appraisers, and consultants of all types. But, it can also be useful for those providing products, as service is a necessary component for gaining product market share.

The book is written from the perspective of an investment advisor entrepreneur because that is where the author gained his experience with the subject matter. The principles contained are readily transferable to anyone wishing to employ skills and talents in his or her own business. Attorneys, accountants, architects, teachers, computer programmers and technicians, medical care professionals, and corporate executives and managers—anyone providing skilled personal services—can benefit from this blueprint to independence. One of the keys to this template is to structure a small business so that it loses little of the clout and resources of a large organization while gaining flexibility of action and personal control over results.

ACKNOWLEDGMENTS

Many people shape us over time. This is an opportunity to thank them. It begins with my parents, Christina and Alfonso Fragasso, the immigrants from Italy who worked so hard to give their son a chance in the new world. And that includes Nick Capelety, also an immigrant, who did the same and was always there for me— my rock and guidepost. From there, special tribute must be given to the Sisters of St. Joseph at St. Canice Elementary School who coped with inner city classes of 45 to 50 children in a post–World War II era and strove to help us overcome our environmental influences and gain the skills necessary to navigate through life. And that transcended to the dedicated teachers of Carrick High School, especially Al Davic, Mike Dimperio, Bill Kohler, Dick Price, and Gabe Verbick, who took up the burden of shaping young people into contributing adults. The traditional and broad educational curriculum of Duquesne University that opened up the world even further for me, along with Fr. Joseph A. Duchene our fraternity chaplain/advisor who taught us how to deal fairly with others, completed my formal education. Thanks also to all of my brothers of Alpha Epsilon fraternity, especially Tony Accamando, Mike Costanzo, Jim Gallagher, Rich Grattan, Jerry Grunert, Jim Linder, Terry McDermott, Larry Novotney, Dave Page, and Steve Yesenosky, who have remained true and supportive friends through all these decades. The "finishing school" touches were administered by the self-sacrificing drill instructors of the U.S. Marine Corps Platoon 3068 at Parris Island, South Carolina. SSgt. J.D. Ramsey, Sgt. B.E. Reese, and Cpl. J.E. Fredendall, thank you wherever you are. I draw on what you taught me about myself every day. Finally, Tom Donaldson, an early supervisor in the business world, was instrumental in setting my course and making me realize my best potential. Without all of that guidance, there would have been no basis for what happened afterward.

Today, a big thank you must go to my business associates at The Fragasso Group, Inc. They are truly a team and enable the success that we enjoy. I also cannot adequately express my appreciation for the supportive association provided by the folks at our strategic partner, Linsco/Private Ledger (LPL). It is impossible to name every one at LPL who has helped us. But, at the forefront are Jim Putnam, Bill Dwyer, and Kandis Bates. And finally, much gratitude goes to Dr. Bob Froehlich, chairman of the Investor Strategy Committee of Scudder Investments, who provided the introduction to the exceptionally professional people at John Wiley and Sons, including my editor, David Pugh, and production editor, Alexia Meyers. Thanks also to Dr. Bob also for writing the forward to this book. Bernie Wetzel, PhD, of Wetzel Consulting and Rick Alfera, CPA, of Goff Backa Alfera were very helpful with the balanced scorecard management system section.

There are so many personal and business friends who influenced me that thanking them would fill an entire book. Please know that you are all appreciated. Every day is an adventure, and I thank every one of the people who participate with me in that exquisite journey.

STARTING YOUR OWN PRACTICE

CHAPTER ONE

IS IT YOUR TIME TO MOVE TO INDEPENDENCE?

Does your current work situation bother you? Does it get to you beyond the ordinary, day-to-day frustrations of working in business or in the professions? If it does, is that caused by the environment in which you work? Or is it caused by the people on whom you depend for new business or for servicing your existing business? Is the revenue or cost sharing unfair? Are your ethics or values in conflict with your employer's?

Do you often ask yourself if you might be more comfortable in a business of your own?

If you are answering, "yes" to any of this, and if your blood pressure is rising while thinking about it, you are a candidate for independence.

But wait before taking action! Let's spend some time on your reasons for wanting business and professional independence. Those reasons will tell you a lot about your chance for success in your potential new venture. And if you do this correctly, this should be your last venture because you will own it. As the saying goes, be careful what you wish for because you may get it. So let's dwell on you and your motivations for a while.

Often, the first thought concerning self-employment deals with money. But rarely do individuals go into business for themselves solely for more income. It is usually more complex than that. See if you can find your feelings in any of the following scenarios:

- The young attorney works hard to bring new business to the firm, and the senior partners do not recognize him for those efforts with an appropriate sharing of the profits or with elevation to partner status. Is that about money, or is it about something more?

- A female certified public accountant (CPA) spends a lot of time on the road representing the firm well in site audits. Meanwhile, her male peer back at the home office has been promoted to supervisor with a hefty raise in salary. Is this just about money?

- And finally, a stockbroker working for a large, national investment firm is pressured to represent his company's internally manufactured products to the exclusion of the independent investment products that are also, ostensibly, offered by his firm. He knows his company has good products, but not all of them are best for his clients. He feels limited in his ability to work ethically on behalf of his clients. That's definitely not about money.

Years ago during the Great Depression, Alfonso Fragasso managed the men's tailoring department for a major department store in Pittsburgh. He had dozens of people working for him and held a prestigious position for a person of his background. He was a master technician who could make a fine suit from a bolt of cloth and also a good manager who was liked and respected by his coworkers. Yet it was the Depression, and the department store's ownership brought in time and motion study people, then called "efficiency experts" to find how to do more with less. Their recommendations, if implemented, would result, in Al's opinion, in diminished quality of goods produced. He also felt it just was not workable because the experts had never done any of the activities they were advocating. He chose to quit rather than oversee what he felt would result in lessened quality and an unworkable situation. It doesn't matter if Al Fragasso was right. He felt he was and acted on it. He spent the rest of his life owning and operating a specialty tailor shop, and he couldn't have been happier. He was well known in his community and respected for the quality of work that he did. And he did it his way.

There is an unspoken word threading through all of these examples and with all of the other examples that we could add to our list. That word is *control*. You do not have to control the company for which you work to feel in control. But if you feel that you are not in control of your outcomes, then you begin to focus on all of the ills that you perceive in your surroundings. If you are bringing in new business to your company but not being compensated or promoted for your efforts, you feel cheated and lacking in control over your destiny. If you see others being promoted for seemingly non-achievement-related reasons, you feel that your career path cannot be influenced by your efforts. You are not in control of those outcomes. If you cannot service your clients ethically and cannot engage in a corporate dialog to rectify it, then you also have no control over your outcomes.

So, what seems to be about money is really about controlling your desired outcomes and guiding your own destiny. True candidates for owning their own business say that they wish to control their own outcomes and destiny—and will earn the income they deserve as a result! So, business ownership is all about deciding which outcomes are desired, how those outcomes are obtained, who helps you do that, in what time frame, and with freedom of ethical action.

THE FINANCIAL BENEFITS

The bonus is that you also control the income you receive for doing it your way—and you build and own the equity in your business. Consider the role that business ownership plays in building wealth. Drs. Thomas Stanley and William Danko examined the accumulation of wealth in their book, *The Millionaire Next Door*. They determined that four out of five U.S. millionaires are still working, while one of the five is retired. Of those still working, two-thirds are self-employed, and 80 percent of those are first-generation affluent and have not received a sizable inheritance. Those folks have six and one-half times the wealth of those not in that category. So there is ample evidence supporting the hypothesis that business ownership is a principal road to wealth and independence. Stanley and Danko state that although self-employed people represent less than 20 percent of the nation's workers, they account for more than 80 percent of the wealth. Average annual income of a business owner is $247,000, and the 50th-percentile median was at $131,000 as of their 1996 writing. And 13 percent of business owners make $500,000 or more. Stanley and Danko peg the average net worth of the successful business owner at $3.7 million with 6 percent of them at more than $10 million.

And you will have lots of company as a business owner. Don't think of small business as a diminishing relic of past generations. Rather, it is a growing trend. The U.S. Small Business Administration published a study in December 2004 using Department of Labor data and covering the period of 1979 through 2003. Self-employed individuals (not incorporated) represented 9.8 percent of the labor force in 2003 versus 9.3 percent of a much smaller labor force in 1979. Their numbers increased by 11.5 million, or 6 percent, in the period between 2000 and 2003. This increase was reflected across both genders and most races. While 9.8 percent of the population is unincorporated self-employed, 6.8 percent of women and 12.4 percent of men are. 10.4 percent of Asian Americans, 5.2 percent of African-Americans, 7.0 percent of Latino-Americans, and 9.9 percent of immigrants are self-employed. Interestingly, while 12.4 percent of men are self-employed, 13.7 percent of male military veterans are self-employed, perhaps representing a higher incidence of marketable skills.

The point of all of these statistics is to present self-employed independence as a viable and growing avenue for marketing skills and for gaining control over one's outcomes and destiny. And that opportunity is not seemingly diminished by gender, race, country of origin, or economic background. A study of incorporated businesses that are controlled by the founder and providing personal services such as legal, accounting, investment management, architectural, and consulting may reflect similar demographics. Anecdotal evidence would indicate so. The research of Stanley and Danko compiled in *The Millionaire Next Door* presents self-employment as a primary road to wealth. And the preceding data indicates the opportunity is available to all, regardless of background.

But you can also become wealthy working for others. You can rise in your field and be paid large sums of money to perform the services that you do well. The U.S. Department of Labor, Bureau of Labor Statistics has published a *National Compensation Survey* listing average earnings for various occupations covering the years 1997 through 2003. In the year 2003, the average corporate nonowner, manager made $71,840; an architect made $62,320, and an accountant made $48,700. Civil engineers averaged $60,440, whereas computer analysts and scientists averaged $66,500. Those are very livable earnings levels, and remember that they are average.

But what happens when workers diligently apply themselves over a career with an employer? What do top people in management and the professions earn? *CareerJournal.com,* the *Wall Street Journal Executive Career Site*, publishes average and top earnings for various occupations. Table 1.1 shows some of their postings in January 2005.

So, if you can earn $100,000 employed by others and not risk your own capital or lose sleep over making payroll, why have your own business? You can also build equity in some one else's business through stock options and other forms of equity incentives offered to you to help your employer build the business. If your primary intent is to earn more income, you can do so with far less risk staying where you are right now and working even harder to progress more quickly within the organization. Be the best architect you can be and, inevitably, your employer or its competitors will recognize that and pay you appropriately. If you become the most productive sales person possible in your chosen field, your employer will have no choice but to pay you commensurately, or lose you to its archrival.

Table 1.1 Typical Earnings from Employers

	Earnings	
Occupation	Average	High
Architect	$54,646	$69,433
Attorney	$72,600	$84,093
Executive	$68,210	$104,970

Why go into business for yourself? Well, if you want to see your idea for a product or a service become a reality, and you want that idea to be implemented in just the right way, your most fulfilling opportunity may be with your own business. If you want to build equity and wealth directly proportional to your efforts, and not wait for someone to eventually recognize your efforts, you must be in business for yourself. If you want to prove yourself, there is no better arena. If you wish to surround yourself with people and a culture of your making, start your own business. You will not have the luxury of specializing your law practice if you work for a large firm. When employed by others, you will spend years, decades or your entire career trying the cases and accepting the clients that your firm dictates to you. As a realtor, you will show the houses and place the mortgages exactly as your supervisor dictates. Your stockbrokerage firm employer will tell just how important the selling from product inventory is to the firm's profits. As a CPA, your firm will dictate your travel schedule and whether or not you will be able to take a vacation day to see your daughter's championship-winning skating performance. As a commercial realtor, you will clearly understand which corporations you may approach and which are off limits as house accounts. *But, as a business owner, you will decide how, when, and with whom your business is conducted. And your earnings will reflect your work, energy, creativity, and your vision.*

In making this decision, there are two questions that you must answer for yourself:

1. What do you want to do each day?
2. With whom do you wish to do it?

Sound simplistic? On the contrary, those questions are both profound and defining. Consider that if you only want to work on highly technical things and not be responsible for gaining new business, you are not a candidate for entrepreneurship. No matter how proficient your skills, people will not beat a path to your door. There actually have been better mousetraps invented. You likely haven't seen them, as everything needs selling and managing. If selling your service to potential clients or customers repulses you, you should not go into business for yourself. Representing your services to potential clients and customers will be required every day and year of your business career. You may not pound doors to tell your story, but you must present it professionally in your daily activities. If that is not what you want to do, then you must leave it to others at your current or a new employment.

A few years ago, a friend was leaving government service as a prosecuting attorney. He was well known and well respected. We had lunch and we spoke of how new business would come to him. It would not come to him simply on the basis of his exemplary government service record. How many people know of that, after all? And how would they know where to find him if they did? He would need to make new business acquisition a part of his daily activities, or he would not prosper. So will you.

So you must first answer the questions of what you want to do each day and with whom before diving into this adventure. This exercise, if performed honestly and fully, may tell you to change your place of employment rather than indicate that you should start your own business. The simple efficiency of this process, using only those two questions, will filter out the background noise provided by family, friends, and the emotional tugs of past associations as well as concerns over adequate capitalization. Although those are substantial considerations that must be properly administered, they are not central to the core decision. Only your uniquely individual answers to those questions will guide you to your self-actualization and career happiness. It will be worth the time spent.

If you determine that you should not be in business for yourself, but still feel unfulfilled in your current situation, you can obtain help through available career counseling services. Seek out psychologists with extensive career counseling experience. Their work with you will help guide you to the right situation. There is a word of caution here. Psychological testing is a commodity. By that I mean any psychologist can administer those tests. But the key is to locate the professional who can interpret the results in a meaningful manner tied to your goals. At our company, we had used various testing facilities for employment evaluations with mixed results. Then a very talented person named Al Schnur bought an agency we had used previously in Pittsburgh, PCI Human Resource Consulting, Inc. The quality of the analytics jumped. We now had a partner who took the time to listen and understand. And that's what you must seek. Find professionals who wish to first listen to your career goals and then account for them in the work they are proposing.

But if your two question exercise of self-exploration points to entrepreneurship and its potential monetary and emotional rewards, keep on reading. The rest of this book is meant to guide you through the design and creation of your business, its implementation, and its successful management.

RISK

Begin with consideration of the risk of business ownership. Might that outweigh the benefits? It probably would not at this point because you have your goal and your reasons for adopting it firmly in mind as a result of your two-question exercise. But it is still worthwhile to spend some time putting risk in perspective and, thus, make it something that you can more easily handle.

The U.S. Small Business Administration in its publication, *Small Business Economics 2003,* referenced Dun & Bradstreet statistics that show 76 percent of new businesses were still open after two years, only 47 percent after four years, and 38 percent after six years. The SBA went on to state in that report that it regularly received calls from alarmed potential entrepreneurs citing the oft-repeated claim that 9 out of 10 new businesses went under, even believing that this occurred in the first year of business. The SBA called this misuse of data a "myth" and attributed its existence to a misunderstanding of generalized statistics. The SBA report stated that the closure statistics also included those businesses "closing while successful." In an SBA study covering 1989 through 1992, 29 percent of closing business owners stated that their companies were successful at time of closing. This would be typical of the otherwise successful service provider (consultant or shoemaker) who wishes to retire and does not have a successor to carry on the business.

Still, risk in business does exist. What factors may lessen risk? The SBA's 2003 report listed very clear success criteria, and that included being mature, properly educated for the business, and having previous experience in the business undertaking. By contrast, gender, race, or even sufficient desire are not meaningful predictors of success. Another large success factor is adequate capitalization. This does not mean that you must have millions of dollars. Having starting capital of even $50,000 dramatically increased the chances of business survival in the SBA study.

So, do not focus too long on generalized statistics that may unfairly sway you from pursuing your life's dream. Instead, spend your time productively evaluating whether independence is the right course for you and arranging the success factors to help make your dream come true.

It lessens risk to stay with what you know. Yes, it is correct that management skills are transferable. But experience should be built on. You are far more likely to succeed as an attorney in building your own law practice than you would be learning to fabricate steel. You can learn the steel business, but why should you? And how much of your precious start up capital will you use while you are trying to catch up the learning curve on your more experienced competitors? So, in that example, fashion a better law firm doing things the way you feel they should be done and servicing the right kind of clients in an innovative way. Practice law over the Internet, create a prepaid legal service for small corporations, or whatever. Be as innovative as you wish, but do it in an arena where your experience-engendered creativity and energy are well placed and most productive.

Finally, risk can be diminished through the use of strategic partnerships. This lessens capital demands and reduces expenses. These partnerships can take many forms, but some of the most common include shared space, personnel, and resources. The most viable would include contracting for skills and resources with established providers instead of creating those resources within the business. Thus, those resources are gained by paying a percentage of the revenue dollar as it is earned rather than creating expense that is constant and ongoing whether or not it is used. An example might be an investment advisor who subcontracts the creation of financial plans or portfolio management to an established provider rather than to incur heavy overhead by hiring and equipping personnel to provide it in-house. Another example would be for an advertising and public relations (PR) firm to subcontract media buying to an independent service rather than to keep a full-time buyer on staff. You determine what may be contracted out to others by determining what activities represent your highest and best use. That is, determine what you provide that is unique to you and that provides your client or customer with a value-added experience. You will make the most money, and incur the least risk, by concentrating on those activities and subcontracting out activities that you can buy cheaply elsewhere. One of the most successful and well-regarded insurance companies in the United States does not provide insurance. It subcontracts the actual insurance underwriting and risk assumption to other companies. Its true value-added experience is its expertise in finding and assessing ideal customers and then servicing them better than other companies can. Consider the overhead it does not incur, and the management focus it gains by concentrating this way and using strategic partners.

In our own firm, we subcontract all of our back-office securities processing and custody to our strategic partner, Linsco/Private Ledger. They specialize in this service, and it would cost us much more of our revenues to try to duplicate it. Plus, we would have at least twice the employees to supervise leaving less time to do what we do best, which is to interact with our clients and watch over their progress toward their financial security.

Another example of strategic partnering is the publishing of this book. Many authors self-publish so that they can gain a higher percentage of the book sales. But that could be limiting. An established publisher, seen as the strategic partner of an author, has the personnel, experience, sales contacts, and clout to sell many more books than the author can while trying to perform all of those duties. So, although the royalties may be less per book, the total books sold will be much greater by using an established strategic partner who knows more than the author can ever hope to learn.

These examples are transferable to almost every endeavor that you may undertake. Your valuable and limited time should be spent doing only your highest and best activities where you uniquely add value. The short-term savings you might expect from trying to do or own it all are illusory when measured against the results you can have from your enterprise when you adhere strictly to your most productive activities. Get an experienced strategic partner for all of the rest.

An added benefit of strategic partnerships is that an under-performing partner can be replaced without going through a corporate downsizing and all that it entails in expense and liability. You can lessen risk considerably by doing only what you do uniquely well and leaving the rest to others. Finally, strategic partnering can allow the smallest companies to compete with the largest with no functional diminishment of resources with which to serve their customers and clients.

THE ENTREPRENEUR'S TEST

Now it is time to take a test to help you decide if self-employment is right for you.

1. Would you do what you are contemplating if someone simply paid your monthly expenses, contributed to your kids' college savings fund and your retirement plan, and nothing more? Would you do it for the sheer fulfillment of seeing your idea come to life?

    What you are looking to do should be so much a part of the fabric of your being that nothing and no one could dissuade you. Remember that it is not about the money. It is all about creating something that actualizes you.

2. Is your spouse or life partner supportive?

    It is very hard to give a new venture your all if you are at odds with the person with whom you share your life. However, this does not translate to blind acceptance of your project by your spouse or partner. He or she should become a valuable reality check resource for you. It is fine to disagree, and the resulting conversations will help shape a better business initiative. But the underlying theme is openness and helpfulness on both sides, not obstructionism.

3. Are you prepared with the necessary skills of your business or profession? And do you possess a necessary understanding of the basics of finance, marketing, and employee management? If not, are you prepared to learn what is needed, and quickly, before embarking?

    It is not necessary to spend years getting ready. But functional and complete training in business management will greatly enhance your chance of success. You may already posses experience and skill. If you don't, get it before starting.

4. Will you be adequately capitalized for the planned endeavor?

    This is a big part of the success formula as the SBA study indicated. Adequate does not have to mean large, just enough. Working with your accountant, you can determine the right amount for identifiable expenses and capital needs as well as a reasonable margin for the unexpected. Making it up as you go is not an acceptable substitute.

5. Can you mentally envision the inevitable tough times that business owners go through and know in your heart that you possess the will to persevere and succeed? And are you ready to do whatever is legal, ethical, and not harmful to your family to make your dream a reality?

    An attitude of "I will not fail" is essential. That is not simply a mantra. It is a firm conviction that you are prepared for your business adventure and are willing to see it through to success. It is fine to feel fear. The legendary underwater explorer, Jacques-Yves Cousteau, wrote in his exciting autobiography that fear is with every brave adventurer. It should not be denied, and is even helpful to make us plan properly and stay alert to danger. So, do not subjugate your fear of the adventure ahead. Use it to your advantage.

If you can honestly answer yes to all five questions, you are a candidate for independence. This book will help you reach your dream. Follow it, stir in your own creativity and energy, and you are on your way to one of life's great adventures. As the Frank Sinatra song says, you will have done it your way. Later, when the business is successful, you will be able to sell it profitably and reap the rewards. Or, maybe you'll have children and grandchildren who will wish to carry on that legacy. Either way, you will have made your mark in the world, helped others realize their dreams, and been rewarded personally and financially for your courage, commitment, perseverance, creativity, and intelligence. That beats being given a gold watch from someone else every time.

CHAPTER TWO

WHAT DOES IT MEAN TO BE IN BUSINESS FOR YOURSELF, AND WHO DOES IT WELL?

Being in business means that you are *responsible* for it all. But that does not mean that you must *do* it all. Proper people management and time management are crucial, as well as organizational ability and the proper use of outside advisors, such as attorneys, accountants, and specialized consultants. Business owners have tremendous time and people demands and are required to make critical judgments in areas where they may not be expert. Knowing how to budget your time and how to hire and grow the right business associates can make the difference between a thriving and an ailing business.

TIME

It is a fallacy that business owners must work 100 hours per week to make their businesses successful. The time requirements for self-employed success are no different from those for a successful paid manager. In *The Millionaire Next Door*, Stanley and Danko's surveys showed that two-thirds of successful business owners work between 45 and 55 hours per week. So do the senior managers and officers of publicly owned companies. Success requires more than 40 hours per week whether you own a business, manage one for someone else, or are a golf pro at a country club. Except for occasional unique times and special projects, working 80 or more hours per week is a symptom of a poor management style. You just can't be consistently productive putting in that many hours week after week. And your personal life will suffer making you even less effective in your business. A later chapter will synthesize techniques for effectively using your time to grow your business without neglecting your own needs or neglecting your family. For now, get ready to put in the business owner's or senior manager's 50- to 55-hour workweek. If you work 55 hours in a week and sleep a full 8 hours each night, you will still have 57 hours left to spend with family and friends, exercise, practice your religion or spirituality, and relax. That represents more than eight hours per day for nonbusiness activities. A successful business does not require sacrificing all else. It does require that you manage which activities you place into your all-important schedule.

There are many books on time management. Most are worth reading and present useful insight. The best of them present a way of thinking rather than an ad hoc collection of time saving ideas. A later chapter dealing with the management of your business and your time contains a distillation of many books and 33 years of study and experience with the subject.

PEOPLE MAKE THE DIFFERENCE

Regardless of the structure of your business, and we will cover that in detail later, you will rely on others to help make your business successful. They will be employees, strategic partners, family, professional advisors, and others providing the infrastructure for your life and business. That includes even your grass cutter and your office building's manager, security guard, and maintenance person. How you make use of them to leverage your own activities and time will help shape your success. Although you rely on these folks, you remain responsible for orchestrating the desired results. You delegate authority and responsibility, but the one responsibility you cannot delegate is that of visioning the future of your company and coordinating the efforts of everyone toward that end. This may be your most critical necessary skill. It requires that you relate well to people and can inspire them to greater accomplishments. It also requires that you understand human nature and are not unduly impacted by periodic, necessary conflict. If you are not able to differentiate and manage this, your business and you will suffer. As with time management, there will be much more on people management as we go through the remainder of the book.

The following is a checklist to gauge how ready you are to take on time and people management as an entrepreneur. If you don't pass the test, it does not mean you are not entrepreneurial material. It simply means that you have to give some thought and generate effort to become ready.

- Can you distinguish the truly important pressures in your life or do you find yourself responding to all of them in equal measure?

- Do you possess an accurate understanding of what are your highest and best uses for your time and effort? Do you clearly see what activities must be delegated to others?

- Are you comfortable with your organizational skills in creating effective delegation and accountability standards for you and your other managers?

- Are you able to stay on task even when being distracted by others or by competing activities?

- Can you list the goals that you have for your business, for your family, and for yourself?

- Do you really like people? Do they usually relate well to you in return?

- Are you unduly influenced by others' opinions rather than simply being open to their ideas?
- Can you articulate a vision and move people to action?

If an honest appraisal has you falling short in some areas, simply understand that you must hone your skills a bit more before embarking on the great adventure of beginning your own business. Books, seminars, and coaching can help. These are the areas of enhanced skill that will help cut your entrepreneurial risk as so much of the success of your business depends on you. Conversely, greater time management and people skills directly translate to greater revenues and profits.

CHAPTER THREE

CREATING YOUR BUSINESS

T his is fun, and it will consume you. Make your plan and enlist everyone you will depend on to make this successful. It will be one of the most exhilarating and trying times of your life. It will take all of your concentration and effort—and will eventually pay you handsomely in money and in satisfaction later. Be aware of the equation that says you will reap what you sow. If you do this correctly, you stand the best chance of success. If you employ haphazard planning and exhibit inattentive implementation, you will appreciably heighten your chance of failure. Or at least you will diminish the return and satisfaction that could have been yours.

The following is the list of activities for your attention. We will devote a section thereafter to each.

- Choose your market niche. You have to have a reason for existing, and it cannot be just because you want your own business.

- Create your business model. How you structure your operation should accurately reflect what you are trying to accomplish and your end goals.

- Plan for staffing and compensation. Who you choose to associate with you will be one of the most crucial of your decisions, and the compensation plan you establish will either steer them toward your business's goals or provide an impediment.

- Establish an action plan and timetable for leaving your current employment and opening your business. Get ready for the D-Day Invasion.

- Evaluate and choose your location and office arrangements. Location, location, location is important, but that doesn't always mean choosing the most expensive arrangement.

- Arrange financing.

- Consider legal format and other security, including business insurance.

- Outline how you will manage your business. This includes everything and everyone in your management and organization structure, even if that's only you, and the outside resources you will employ.

- Determine your fallback positions and exit strategy. This should be accomplished as a positive exercise to perpetuate the business and not to build a bridge back to your former existence. You must burn the landing boats at the beach once you have decided to invade this new land. Your mind must be turned forward, but, that does not mean that you should not consider contingency adjustment plans.

- Organize all of the necessary action steps and the timeline for starting your business in conformity with everything you have just outlined. This will be the real test of your organizational skills as well as your dedication and perseverance. Done correctly, it will carry you through to your business startup goal.

Now let's explore each of these areas in depth.

CHOOSING YOUR MARKET NICHE

The world is not waiting for you to start your business. But it may welcome you with open arms once it sees what you have to offer. The reality is that you will have to work hard to clearly identify the value that you are bringing to the marketplace. You must then decide how to market and advertise your unique value so that people will want it. It doesn't matter how much skill you possess. It can't be sold if the buyer hasn't been conditioned to value it. Start with the segment of the market that you believe will value what you offer.

There are few industries more heavily populated with competition than the financial services industry. It is also very fragmented. Large, national stock brokerage firms offer financial products, as do insurance companies and banks. There are independent financial advisors and companies that specialize in portfolio management. How to choose the right advisor is a constant dilemma for individuals and retirement-plan trustees who need to guide themselves and the assets entrusted to them to financial success. The same can probably be said of your industry. How would you differentiate yourself from the herd, justify the existence of your company, and attract new business, especially in the face of such a myriad of well-financed competitors?

Start by articulating for yourself in the planning stages what you can do uniquely. In the financial services industry, as well as in others, it might be relating on a personalized basis with clients and taking an all-inclusive guidance approach with them. The monolithic firms cannot accomplish that nearly as well. Another unique, value-added niche may be to offer your services without proprietary product bias as you are working for the client and not the product-creating company. It may be that you, for example, craft individualized financial plans for clients before investing their money in accordance with the needs identified in that analysis and plan. That will differentiate you from the companies who show the same products to all regardless of the client's circumstances. It also will set your methodology above that of the planner who sends off a cursorily completed data input form to a faceless, mindless computer at the home office to get back a standardized plan that could fit any number of people. Many management books, going all the way back to Sun Tzu and the *Art of War*, have advocated the exploitation of your competitor's weaknesses. The corollary is to position your strengths in relation to those weaknesses. Those strengths and weaknesses will not be apparent to your marketplace. You might feel that they should, but people will not focus that closely unless you help them understand.

You must conceptualize your value-added differences and then communicate them effectively to any prospective client or customer in a way that makes them want what you are offering. It may also be that you possess specialized skills, such as a sparsely practiced or a specialized area of the law or special use architecture. By definition, this would encompass a smaller marketplace so that you still must be prepared to accentuate your value proposition to gain some of the existing market as well as potentially create new market demand. Concentrate on what you do better, more ethically, faster, or more beneficially different from the competition if you wish to be successful in your business.

But, be careful of two areas of risk. Do not directly bash your competition. You will only serve to lessen your stature and the perception of your industry in the eyes of your prospective customer or client. And, above all, do not set yourself apart by price alone. There will always be someone willing to do your kind of work cheaper than you. If your client deals with you solely as the lowest cost provider, you will lose them eventually. There is also an association of lowest cost with lesser quality. This often dooms you to deal only with the cost conscious customer who can least afford you and often causes the most headaches over credit and service dissatisfaction. Consider the phrase, "price is an issue only in the absence of value." That does not mean that you can price yourself noncompetitively, but, it does indicate that you can price your services fairly and in line with the true value that you furnish. Usually that means you can be squarely in the middle of the pack for your industry in pricing. It then becomes an issue of proper business model structure and implementation to make that price profitable for you.

Take the time now to make a list of all the things that make you and your service special in your marketplace. Use the following list as a guide, but do not limit yourself to it. Here's where your experience, your understanding of your industry and your competitors, and your creativity will pay off.

- Who are the major players in my industry and in my locality?

- What common threads run through their business delivery models?

- What can I offer in a better way?

- What segments of the marketplace are not being adequately served by my major competition?

- How can I provide my services more efficiently, faster, or with less cost and/or greater perceived value?

- Who are the best people or entities to help me get my message of enhanced value across to the marketplace?

- What are the possible conflicts of interest built into my major competitors' business models that I might exploit?

- Are there ways to price my service that are different, but not necessarily cheaper, than my major competition so as to make my pricing model more attractive to clients or customers?

STRUCTURING YOUR BUSINESS TO SERVE YOUR MARKET NICHE

Every business has a *sales continuum* that looks like this.

Generate leads→Lead becomes prospect→Prospect becomes client→Service client→Client refers to new prospects

You will need to complete this exercise for your business or profession. As an illustrative exercise, we will use a financial advisory firm example to learn how it is to be done. First, we will list all of the choices possible for each step and then narrow those down to what suits our marketplace, our skills, and our personal preferences for doing business.

Generate Leads	Lead to Prospect	Prospect to Client
Cold call by phone	Exploratory meeting	Convince to do business
Cold call in person	Hope to gain appointment	Convince to do business
Dinner lectures at hotel	Meet with anyone who schedules	Convince to do business
Advertise heavily for leads	Call for exploratory meeting	Convince to do business
Direct mail solicitation	Mail requested literature and call for exploratory meeting	Convince to do business
Network with other professionals and acquaintances	Follow up for names to contact and arrange exploratory meeting	Convince to do business
Educational seminars	Demonstrate professional competence in a non-commercial and non-threatening setting	Have attendees self-select to meet with me as a problem solver. Build a mechanism into the seminars that fosters that.

As I view the lead generating technique possibilities, my industry experience tells me cold calling is a better way to gain poise than it is to gain clients. So I reject that.

Dinner lectures at hotels and clubs can gain leads, but they are expensive and tend to attract less favorable prospects. Also, the sales pitch over dinner to strangers is not the image I want to project. I may do dinner lectures later for established clients and their invited guests as a client appreciation educational outreach. That can be part of turning client servicing into referred leads, but it's not as potent with strangers.

Advertising is also costly and, based on my experience in the industry, I know that even the largest and most cash heavy firms can not depend on that as a reliable source of new business. I know that it creates awareness and I may use it for that purpose later in conjunction with other more direct outreach initiatives. But alone it will not bring me the prospects that I need.

Direct mail solicitation can be effective, but costly. Another problem is that it usually is product oriented, and I have determined that I want to be an advisor, not a product salesperson. That is one of the ways I decided to differentiate myself from the herd of investment product purveyors, so the idea of a mass mailing to folks, whose individual needs are unknown, is discarded. I may, however, choose to use direct mail for a specially selected audience, such as retirement plan or endowment fund trustees where I can more narrowly tailor my message to their known needs.

Networking can be very effective, and I will always incorporate it with other outreaches. But my experience tells me that networking cannot be my sole method for gaining leads.

By process of elimination, I have settled on educational seminars because I know them to be effective. This way of gaining prospects for my services is lower in cost than other alternatives, and it fits the image that I want to present. I like the idea that prospective clients can prejudge me in a noncommercial and unthreatening environment. I know from my previous work that an educated client makes better and easier decisions and is more fun to work with. Educational seminars are then coupled with subsequently gaining referrals from my clients and networking with compatible professionals serving the same marketplace. I can also network within business and social groups.

You should completely cover for yourself the four stages of gaining clients: (1) lead generation, (2) turning leads to prospects, and (3) turning prospects to clients. From there, (4) go on to establishing service standards for clients and implant steps into those service standards that create client referrals as a natural outcome rather than as an uncomfortable, hesitating, and lurching by-product. Your sales continuum will then be complete.

Begin by brainstorming ideas for lead generation and then narrow down the alternatives to what best fits you and your market. The details are then filled in as to action steps, time-line, and resources needed. This methodology is carried on through the remaining steps of the sales continuum to create an entire business plan.

Consider the alternative to analyzing and planning your marketing strategy: Open your doors for business and hope. That is not a better alternative. If you plan well and faithfully execute your plan, you will have a much better chance of things happening the way you wish.

Take the sale continuum and begin filling in your business's details.

Leads→Prospects→Clients→
Servicing Clients→Referred prospects

Then list all of the possible action steps that you might employ in each stage of the continuum.

Next, weed out the steps that seem less productive or that do not conform to your desired way of operating.

Now you are ready to begin fashioning your basic marketing and management plan. This will also help guide you to a proper expression of the true value that you can offer to clients.

Leo Pusateri in his book, *Mirror Mirror on the Wall, Am I the Most Valued of Them All?* provides a blueprint for creating and drafting a complete expression of your unique value to be presented both verbally and in print to clients. The following is what his value ladder looks like:

Client Question	**Expression of Value**
Why should I do business with you?	Real value
What makes you different?	Differentiation
Who have you done it for?	Client successes
How do you do what you do?	Process
Why do you do what you do?	Business beliefs
What do you do?	Unique value proposition
Who are you?	Background

It is imperative that you answer the questions beginning at the bottom and then rising by steps to the top rung of the ladder. You must answer those questions from the perspective of your potential client and in a succinct and meaningful way that allows for a quick but complete understanding of the value you can add to a client's life. If you can't, every encounter is hit or miss, and you lessen your chances of success. If you can create your unique value ladder, you will gain the obvious advantage over your competition. But very importantly, this process will form the framework for your personal services practice. It will guide every decision from staffing to advertising. It will guide you to the type of clients that you should accept and help you identify those who are not a good fit. Rather than limit your success, it will accelerate you along the road as you focus on your highest and best uses and allow you to intelligently articulate your value to those who should hear it.

This exercise should begin with a brief statement answering each of the questions. Then take those answers and create a statement that is phrased from the perspective of your client. Your entire team should participate in the creation of those statements for two important reasons.

1. You will have the most complete statement possible. No one person, regardless of intellect, can equal the quality of scrutiny that an experienced team can provide in this exercise. The more diverse the views, the better the end result once they have all been melded into a comprehensive statement.

2. By involving the entire team, you gain buy-in for the use of the end result with your prospects and clients. This beneficial use is much more assured than if you created it and then fostered in on everyone else.

For illustration, view the initial answers that our firm might give to those questions to help you get started on your exercise. Remember that this stage of phraseology is but a start. Once all of the phrases have been compiled in answer to the questions, you and your team must craft them into succinct and impactful answers phrased from the perspective of a client. This is for both internal and external use, so it has to be meaningful to your associates and your clients. Also remember to start at the bottom of the ladder and work to the top. Take the time to go through Pusateri's book for comprehensive instruction on this process.

Why should I do business with you?

(Real value: *Why should I trust you?*)

We have attempted to earn your trust by engineering potential conflicts of interest from our relationship: no sales commissions, proprietary products, inventories, or underwritings.

Our fee versus commission structure places us on your side. If your assets grow, so does our fee.

Our role is to guide you through to your successful financial future. We give objective measurement quarterly and annually to help you know we are on track together.

Our firm is managed by a group of four managing directors, so its continuance is not dependent on any one individual.

Collectively, our financial consultants and portfolio managers have more than 200 years of industry experience.

Our web site and published material contain each of our direct dial phone numbers and direct-to-PC e-mail addresses. The president's home phone number is in the telephone book. We are here for you.

We have better than a 99 percent client retention rate through good and bad economic periods

What makes you different?

(Differentiation)

Our employees are compensated by salary and a sharing of total firm revenues and profits. None are on commission.

We represent no proprietary products, so we work for the client not the product manufacturer.

We have no inventories nor do we underwrite initial public offerings of securities so as to avoid potential conflicts of interest.

We manage accounts for clients individually and not on a commingled basis. This allows for management by individual goals and risk level.

We manage accounts internally with a dedicated portfolio management team. You will meet with your portfolio manager along with your relationship manager.

Portfolio management is financially incentivized to provide you with good performance.

You will receive personalized attention and communication by individuals you know.

Whom have you done business with?

(Client successes)

Industry ethics and regulations often preclude the identification of clients. Even when this not prohibited, it's not usually a good idea to name clients publicly. We answer this question in two ways: first, by category of client such as

- Individuals
- Retirement plans
- Endowment funds

Second, we have created client profiles that do not name the client. Instead, they are reflected by their occupations or stage of life, such as

- Entrepreneur
- Corporate executive
- Woman business owner
- Retired couple
- Corporate retirement plan
- College endowment fund

How do you do what you do?

(Process)

We use a comprehensive analysis of the individual's or business's situation coupled with an understanding of the client's goals.

We make comprehensive recommendations based on that analysis.

We offer complete management of the investment assets and guidance for all of the aspects of the client's financial circumstances.

We continually monitor investments and progress toward financial and life goals.

We provide communication in writing and with measurable performance and life planning schedules as needed on a quarterly and annual basis.

We offer annual comprehensive review meetings with clients.

Why do you do what you do?   **(Business beliefs)**

We believe that owning a stake in the capital assets of the United States and world economies is integral to long term financial security.

Textbook principles of investment and financial management are the best guides. We avoid trendy and faddish methodologies.

Investment management is best accomplished individually for each client through a thorough evaluation of the client's goals, objectives, family and business structure, time frames, and risk tolerance level.

What do you do?

(Unique value proposition)

We provide management of investment assets on a fee basis, based on a platform of comprehensive financial planning and asset allocation modeling.

Who are you?

(Background)

We have been in business for 33 years through all market and business cycles.

We are a team of 24 individuals with distinct and complimentary disciplines—portfolio management, estate planning, financial planning, education funding expertise, and risk management.

We are licensed in 33 states with clients in several foreign countries.

Remember that these are only thoughts that speak to the questions. From here we must fashion our value statement for each rung of the ladder to enable a smooth and efficient translation of those facts and beliefs in writing as well as in conversation.

Now, you might read our answers to the questions and respond, "But of course! Who would say differently?" The fact is that many financial advisors would respond differently because there are many methodologies for providing financial advice and investment management. These statements clearly differentiate us. Worse, many advisors would not be able to say anything beyond some cursory phraseology and platitudes. They know what they do, but they are unprepared to articulate a comprehensive and client-centric description of the value they bring. Can you? You will once you complete this exercise for yourself.

CREATING YOUR ORGANIZATIONAL MODEL

Now that you have defined the unique value proposition for your practice, your next step is to identify the structural model that will best facilitate your activities. For the personal service provider, there are three basic structural configurations.

1. James Bond, secret agent
2. The college rathskeller
3. Special operations (ops) team

James Bond, Secret Agent

This is the most common design for the personal service provider. It eventually becomes self-defeating. When you view the typical attorney, accountant, financial advisor, and architect, you find the competent practitioner who develops clientele and pretty much does it all. James Bond can do everything and only needs tangential administrative support from Miss Moneypenny and some technical support from Q. That means all strings are connected to James and nothing can advance unless he makes it happen. That is why it is termed self-defeating.

It can be the appropriate model for someone who wishes to remain in that role for his or her entire career, and that does not make this a bad choice. But to grow, that person must add more Moneypennies and more Qs. The burden of supervision in such a precipitously vertical structure will begin to erode the time available for doing the very work for which the service provider is best paid and for which the business was originally started. This is the model that is normally seen when personal service providers first go into business for themselves. It is logical for that stage of their careers and is the least costly. Eventually a growth decision must be made and an early awareness of that makes for an easier transition later.

The College Rathskeller

This model may also be found at the onset of the business or later in the growth phase. It usually is adopted to spread fixed costs, like rent and administrative help, among many. Recall that Miss Moneypenny did not work only for James. Now remember back to the student union at college where everyone hung out at the rathskeller. Everyone did similar things and drew from the same set of resources, housing, food, utilities, and even communication. But they were not mutually dependent and, if one person dropped out, the rest went on with their own lives and activities.

This model is often seen in a large investment or real estate brokerage firm or other professional firm. The coming and leaving of associates is of general interest, but does not materially impact the remaining providers. Also, gaining new business is often an individual affair, and loose arrangements for partnering are made and broken. This model serves best when independent service providers wish to share common resources to share costs, whether that be investment research, communication systems, or libraries of information, as well as rent and secretarial help. But very often, turf battles break out and negate the nebulous benefits derived from cost sharing. There is rarely synergy arising from everyone's efforts. Beyond sharing rent costs and the occasional water cooler or lunchtime social conversation, you could not care less what the others are doing or even if they are there at all. And sometimes the presence of quasi-competing influences can act as a retardant on your personal production. This may be your scenario now and that may be why you are considering moving to an independent model. You will want to consider well before implementing this model in your new business.

The Special Ops Team

Here the personal service provider acts as the team leader with a complete array of specialists to handle the various duties necessary to gain clients, service them, and turn those relationships into referrals to more clients. This allows business owners to fulfill only their highest and best uses and that is the reason that they went into business for themselves originally. Several other very tangible benefits accrue from this model.

The client or customer feels well serviced. Imagine, by contrast, customers walking into the workplace of a rathskeller model threading through the myriad indifferent or predatory stares of the other agents or professionals to find the work areas or offices of their service providers. By contrast, in the special ops model, a team member who is vitally interested in the client's satisfaction warmly greets the client at the door. The client knows, for example, that an assigned portfolio manager and a dedicated administrative person support the financial consultant and that another financial consultant is both knowledgeable and available in the primary contact's absence.

The professional service provider is secure in an environment free of internal competition and benefits from mutual support among team members. There is freedom to schedule family time, vacation time, and personal development training, knowing that clients or customers will be well served and a professional posture presented in the principle's absence.

The advantage to business owners is that they own a business rather than it owning them. Michael Gerber offers a well-examined analysis of this concept in his book, *The E-Myth Revisited: Why Most Small Businesses Don't Work and What to Do about It.* The special ops team approach allows the owner a reasonable quality of life by allocating time for work, family, and personal growth and enjoyment. This book could never have been written if the author had retained a James Bond business model and failed to implement a team approach to business.

A significant additional benefit to the owner occurs at the sale of the business or at the time of transfer to the next generation of family ownership. Business valuation specialists place a premium on businesses and professional practices that are not dependent on the owner's constant and continued presence. If the clients or customers tie their perception of value to the owner's skills alone, there could be considerable exodus of clients at time of sale or at the retirement of the owner. If you only know and value James Bond's work and skills, you may look for a replacement elsewhere when James retires to the islands. If instead, the owner stresses the client value inherent in the team, the transition to new or successor ownership offers a much better chance of higher client or customer retention. The owner may balk at this as it may, at first look, diminish his stature or influence with clients. But the opposite is true. Clients appreciate the added security of the team approach. And the owner's foresight and

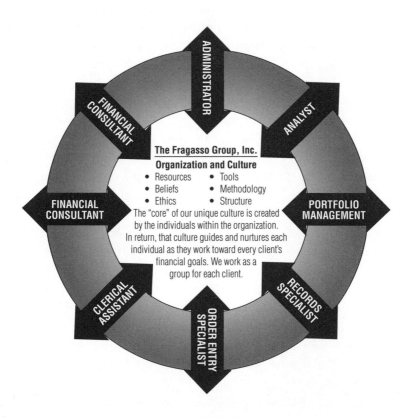

Figure 3.1 Organizational and Cultural Model

skill in creating an efficient team model makes the owner more valued than a harried and overworked sole service provider. Sometimes owners take longer than they should to get over the ego problem involved in this evolutionary process, but, once accomplished, they see and benefit from the heightened stature and greater efficiency that their ego sublimation allowed them to create.

Our graphic representation of our special ops team is a wheel with spokes and is included in our client and prospect literature (see Figure 3.1). We believe it makes those folks feel much more comfortable with us than if we were structured as an owner-centric organization. Note that the core of our wheel is our firm's culture and not any one individual as would be the case with a James Bond-type business model. The spokes have arrows pointed in both directions to signify that every individual contributes to the creation of our culture and that each person is bound by that culture. We also point out that the group's intent is to push the wheel in the same direction so as to achieve positive motion.

CHAPTER FOUR

STAFFING AND COMPENSATION

This subject fills many books. We will view it from its essence relative to starting your own business or professional practice. You cannot decide on staffing or compensation until you have adopted one of the three business models described in Chapter 3. For example, if the rathskeller model seems best, you will want to do an analysis of the overhead cost necessary to support independent contractors or commission service providers housed in your business. Then you will determine the correct revenue and cost sharing allocation. If you are utilizing the James Bond model, you will probably use a combination of salary and some sort of incentive compensation geared to the type of support you expect from your administrative and technical people. Finally, the special ops approach requires a combination of a dependable salary level and sharing of total firm or team revenue. To employ any other method is to work against your desired aims. If you compensate team members based only on their own area's productivity, they will have no incentive to help other team members. Departmental factionalism will prevail over the firm's needs. But with firm-wide or team-wide shared compensation, all members care mightily about client satisfaction stemming from all areas and departments because everyone's incentive compensation depends on all team members servicing the client well.

The potential drawback to this approach is that weaker team members could be carried along on the backs of those who work more diligently. In a smaller company, that problem is more apparent than real because everyone knows who is not pulling their full weight. Because everyone depends on everyone else, like in a military special ops team, everyone has a personal stake in helping or encouraging weaker members to rise to expectations. If they refuse, the other team members will frankly not allow the laggards to continue. Weaker team members grow through team training and mentoring, or they are removed if they refuse to grow. This potential problem becomes more an issue of proper management than one of compensation.

This management challenge can be readily addressed by instituting a third level of compensation, which we term our personal evaluation program (PEP). This allows team or departmental managers to work with team members on a quarterly basis collaboratively setting individual goals that address areas for improvement or enhanced skills. It can be as simple as an improved typing level or as involved as gaining another professional designation. Long-term goals should be broken up into manageable, quarterly subgoals meant to accomplish the objective along a predetermined timetable. This third level of compensation does not have to be as large as the incentive compensation where firm-wide revenues are shared. Its existence alone offers sufficient motivation to higher levels of achievement. Although a PEP quarterly bonus is a confidential matter between team member and manager, no members wish to receive zero bonus or even 80 percent of what they could have enjoyed. The ideal way to begin a PEP program is to grant 100 percent of the PEP bonus during the first quarter of the program's existence. It is not attractive to team members to be granted a diminished bonus thereafter for subpar performance. Employees are therefore motivated to continue the previous bonus level by achieving the collaboratively identified personal achievement goals for the next quarter and thereafter. No one wishes to explain to a spouse or life partner why the quarterly bonus went down.

The PEP can be powerful if used correctly. It is advisable to have professional assistance in structuring it initially because a poorly constructed or unfairly implemented plan will demotivate rather than inspire team members. In Pittsburgh, we used an experienced human relations and management consultant, Ray Amelio, for our program.

Ray has decades of experience with employee evaluation and compensation. You will not want to skimp on experienced, professional advice in this area because the success of your enterprise depends heavily on your team members.

We use similar PEP evaluation sheets for managers and for nonmanagers. The manager's PEP is reproduced here. We simply remove the ending managerial section for nonmanagers. Notice that a preparation section exists for each employee or associate to complete prior to the evaluation meeting along with the sheets for the manager's detailed evaluation of the employee. This joint preparatory work reinforces the importance of the exercise and helps ensure mutual participation.

FRAGASSO GROUP
Manager Performance Evaluation

EMPLOYEE NAME: _____

DEPARTMENT:_____

POSITION TITLE: _____

MANAGER CONDUCTING APPRAISAL: _____

PART I—PERFORMANCE FACTORS—20 PERCENT

Carefully review the employee's work performance in relation to the current job description. Please check the appropriate level to indicate the employee's performance. The rankings for the individual performance factors will correspond to the following: **Exceeds requirements, Meets requirements, Needs improvement, and Unsatisfactory.** Please provide specific examples/incidents or describe patterns of performance to support your evaluation.

JOB KNOWLEDGE: Knowledge of job gained through experience, education, and specialized training. Degree of familiarity with regular job duties.

❑ Very effective and thorough knowledge of all phases of job function and its relation to other jobs. **(Exceeds requirements)**

(continued)

❏ Understands major phases of the job. **(Meets requirements)**

❏ Noticeable deficiencies in job knowledge. **(Needs improvement)**

❏ Unsatisfactory knowledge of job. **(Unsatisfactory)**

Comments:

_____

_____

_____

_____

_____

PROFESSIONAL IMAGE: Projects a professional image through appearance and/or conduct appropriate to the position.

❏ Consistently projects exemplary appearance and/or conduct. **(Exceeds requirements)**

❏ Appearance and/or conduct are acceptable. **(Meets requirements)**

❏ Appearance and/or conduct need improvement. **(Needs improvement)**

❏ Appearance and/or conduct are unsatisfactory. **(Unsatisfactory)**

Comments:

_____

_____

_____

_____

_____

PLANNING AND ORGANIZING: Level of effectiveness in determining strategies to achieve goals and objectives.

❏ Consistently effective in establishing and organizing priorities, coordinating activities, and communicating with others, both internally and externally. **(Exceeds requirements)**

❑ Effectively coordinates activities, establishes priorities, and communicates these to others, both internally and externally. **(Meets requirements)**

❑ Has difficulty in organizing workflow to comply with priorities. **(Needs improvement)**

❑ Ineffective in establishing priorities and coordinating activities. **(Unsatisfactory)**

Comments:

_____

_____

_____

_____

_____

DECISION MAKING: Ability to arrive at sound decisions with positive results.

❑ Consistently weighs available information making very sound decisions and recommendations. **(Exceeds requirements)**

❑ Achieves good results through sound decisions and recommendations. **(Meets requirements)**

❑ Reluctant to make decisions. Decisions are not always sound. **(Needs improvement)**

❑ Ineffective in making decisions and recommendations. **(Unsatisfactory)**

Comments:

_____

_____

_____

_____

_____

(continued)

INITIATIVE: Ingenuity, self-reliance, resourcefulness, assertiveness, ambition, and ability to know what needs to be done. Ability to take needed action without direct instructions.

❏ A self-starter, resourceful in situations with good follow-through. Recognizes and often recommends solutions. **(Exceeds expectations)**

❏ Accepts opportunity to increase value of job or personal contribution once supervisory instruction is given. **(Meets requirements)**

❏ Follows established pattern of doing job without innovation. **(Needs improvement)**

❏ Resists change. Slow to get started. Allows projects to lag after starting and requires direct supervision. **(Unsatisfactory)**

Comments:

_____

_____

_____

_____

_____

_____

A. COMMUNICATION SKILLS: Ability to clearly exchange information, both written and oral. Consider listening skills as a key component of this performance capacity.

❏ Very effective communicator. Both oral and written communication skills are above average with all levels of personnel. **(Exceeds requirements)**

❏ Effective in communicating ideas in written and verbal form. **(Meets requirements)**

❏ Communications are generally clear and concise, but at times employee requires assistance in selecting subject matter and audience for the information. **(Needs improvement)**

❏ Verbal and/or written communication is often unclear and misunderstood. **(Unsatisfactory)**

Comments:

_____

_____

_____

_____

_____

TEAMWORK AND COOPERATION: Maintains a positive approach, accepts policies, demonstrates a constructive response to criticism, and works with others as an integral team member.

❏ Self-confident and effective in dealing with all levels of people. Weighs other viewpoints objectively and gains acceptance from others. **(Exceeds requirements)**

❏ Adjusts to situations and readily accepts new ideas and changes. Is tactful and accepts criticism without difficulty. **(Meets requirements)**

❏ May make an adequate adjustment to situations but may not always be as tactful as the situation requires. May create problems for others without realizing it. **(Needs improvement)**

❏ Does not interact well with others. **(Unsatisfactory)**

Comments:

_____

_____

_____

_____

_____

B. MANAGEMENT SKILLS: COMPLETE THE FOLLOWING IF APPLICABLE TO THE POSITION.

LEADERSHIP/DELEGATION: Effectiveness in accomplishing actions through others. Consider how well employee delegates responsibility while retaining accountability.

(continued)

❑ Consistently effective in assigning responsibilities and using judgment in analyzing capabilities of others to complete objectives. **(Exceeds requirements)**

❑ Generally obtains cooperation from others and usually gets the job done on time. Assigns responsibility and authority and directs the activities of others in an acceptable manner. **(Meets requirements)**

❑ Often has difficulty in getting the job done through others. Prefers to do the job personally and does not provide adequate or complete instruction/direction. **(Needs improvement)**

❑ Ineffective in delegating and directing the activities of others. **(Unsatisfactory)**

Comments:

_____

_____

_____

_____

APPRAISE PERFORMANCE/COACH AND COUNSEL EMPLOYEES: Objectively prepares and conducts appraisals; ability to conduct effective counseling/coaching sessions with employees.

❑ Very effective in judging performance level of staff and counseling/coaching for employee development. Encourages feedback and establishes an open channel of communication. **(Exceeds requirements)**

❑ Objectively analyzes staff performance and capabilities; coaches/counsels with staff as needed. **(Meets requirements)**

❑ Needs to improve in the accuracy and/or timeliness of appraising and coaching/counseling staff. **(Needs improvement)**

❑ Ineffective in accurately appraising and coaching/counseling staff. **(Unsatisfactory)**

Comments:

_____

_____

_____

_____

C. PART II—PERFORMANCE GOALS—80 PERCENT

Establish performance goals for the next review period. Include completion dates. Please use additional sheets if more room is needed.

Goals Completion Date
Note: Goals should be **SMART**
(**S**pecific, **M**easurable, **A**chievable, **R**elevant, **T**ime-bound)

1. **Date**
2. **Date**
3. **Date**
4. **Date**
5. **Date**
6. **Date**
7. **Date**
8. **Date**

PART III—TRAINING NEEDS

Please discuss with the employee any training needs. These needs may be identified as gaps between existing and desired competencies or skills, current and desired job performance, or what the Fragasso Group expects to happen and what actually happens. Please use additional sheets if more room is needed.

PART IV—CAREER OBJECTIVES

Please discuss with the employee and comment on the employee's career aspirations (not necessarily a specific position) and/or desire for further job development.

I. ADDITIONAL COMMENTS

MANAGER/SUPERVISOR _____

EMPLOYEE _____

Employee is encouraged to use this space to comment on areas of agreement/disagreement with this appraisal. If additional space is needed, please attach separate comment pages to this appraisal.

(continued)

Employee's Signature _____ Date_____

Appraising Manager's
Signature _____ Date_____

Employee's signature acknowledges that the appraisal was discussed with the employee. It does not imply agreement or disagreement with the appraisal.

PERFORMANCE APPRAISAL PREPARATION FORM

EMPLOYEE NAME: _____

DATE: _____

To help you prepare for your upcoming performance evaluation, please provide written comments for each performance factor that reflects your evaluation of your performance during the past year. Also reflect on your performance goals for the year and write down how you believe you performed against the goals that were established at the beginning of this appraisal year.

PERFORMANCE FACTORS

JOB KNOWLEDGE—How well do you know your job?

Comments:

_____

_____

_____

_____

PROFESSIONAL IMAGE—Is your professional image through your appearance and conduct appropriate to the position?

Comments:

_____

_____

_____

_____

PLANNING AND ORGANIZING—How effective are you in planning and organizing ways to achieve results?

Comments:

_____

_____

_____

_____

_____

DECISION MAKING—Evaluate your ability to arrive at sound decisions

Comments:

_____

_____

_____

_____

_____

INITIATIVE—Evaluate your ability to take needed action without direct instructions.

Comments:

_____

_____

_____

_____

_____

(continued)

COMMUNICATION—Evaluate your ability to clearly exchange information both orally and in writing.

Comments:

_____

_____

_____

_____

_____

TEAMWORK AND COOPERATION—Evaluate your ability to maintain a positive approach, accept policies and procedures, receive constructive criticism, and work with others as a team.

Comments:

_____

_____

_____

_____

_____

MANAGEMENT SKILLS

LEADERSHIP/DELEGATION—Evaluate your effectiveness in accomplishing actions through others while retaining accountability.

Comments:

_____

_____

_____

_____

_____

APPRAISE PERFORMANCE/COACH AND COUNSEL EMPLOYEES—Do you objectively prepare and conduct employee performance appraisals? Evaluate your ability to effectively coach and counsel employees when required.

Comments:

_____

_____

_____

_____

_____

FILLING POSITIONS IN YOUR MODEL WITH THE RIGHT PEOPLE

You have decided on your business model from among the secret agent, rathskeller, or special ops team choices. And you have appropriately structured your compensation methodology to coincide with that model. You can now decide what positions you will need to fill to run your business properly. That task becomes easy once the structure is in place. If you are in secret agent mode, you simply decide what administrative and technical duties of your operation others should perform, write job descriptions, and hire and pay accordingly. If adopting a rathskeller model, you must decide what common services and infrastructure you will provide to the associates and then locate persons for those positions. You will also need to spell out the revenue and cost sharing arrangements for the rathskeller professionals.

The special ops team works similarly, but this configuration requires the highest degree of attention in structuring the positions and in hiring because of the enormous amount of interdependence among team members. As in a military context, mission achievement will only occur through a well-integrated and coordinated team. They must trust each other and know that respective tasks will be accomplished without the need for cajoling or, as we like to say, "diapering and powdering." If one team member is to hold the rope, so to speak, while another member climbs, the climber cannot be distracted in wondering if the rope holder is really there holding the rope or if he or she tied it to a bush while off somewhere else. Also, cooperation and team spirit are required. In a rathskeller model, one seeks the most proficient practitioner, and a cooperative personality is not essential, although always desirable. But in a team, a cooperative personality is required for successful team functioning. We once employed a very talented individual who had very sharp elbows. He used them to move his fellow team members aside and take personal credit for team accomplishments. Pronouns in his conversation were always personal and singular. He never used plural pronouns in his speech or gave credit to others. These practices were symptomatic of his inability to function in team. Although we tried very hard to adjust his way of interacting, it was never going to be a part of his style. We now interview and test for the ability to sublimate personal ego for team accomplishment. And you should also if you adopt the team business model.

YOUR FRINGE BENEFIT PACKAGE AS A RECRUITMENT, RETENTION, AND PRODUCTIVITY TOOL

Compensation includes more than salaries and bonuses. Your fringe benefit package will become a useful tool in attracting and retaining valuable associates. When you hire employees or associates of any type, you take on some degree of responsibility for their success. And as they are aligning their future with that of your company, you assume responsibility for providing appropriate personal resources so that all employees or associates can work to maximum capability and provide for their families. Thusly, the range of compensation and benefit considerations includes the following:

- Salary and bonuses
- Retirement plans

- Life insurance

- Disability insurance

- Health insurance

- Vacation, sick, and personal days

- Cafeteria fringe benefit options

- Wellness education and opportunities

- Pretax savings accounts for health, child care, and transportation costs

- Job and skills training

- Job-related tools and resources

- Individual achievement awards

We have covered salary, bonuses, and individual performance awards. It is worth considering the other components of your compensation package because they are integral to recruiting, retention, and productivity. People want to work where they feel valued. It is not necessary for you to have the most generous retirement plan matching program in town, but you must have a retirement plan and other such fringe benefits so that your people will view your firm as a career opportunity. The subtle costs of frequent turnover and lack of employee focus to results are both real and significant. Here are some thoughts on each of the preceding fringe benefits for your consideration.

RETIREMENT PLANS

Employees are used to contributing to their own retirement savings in the form of 401K plans. It is not necessary or expected, especially in personal service businesses, to have a costly defined benefit pension plan. Defined contribution plans such as 401K, SEP IRA, and others are readily available and can be installed at relatively reasonable cost. Enlist your accountant and financial advisor to help determine what you can afford and which plan best suits your goals for your company. Do not neglect employee financial education. This should be available to you without additional cost by the provider of the retirement plan package.

LIFE INSURANCE

Life insurance is relatively low cost when done on a group basis. Employees are also preconditioned to contribute toward the premiums. In a typical configuration, the company provides one times salary to a maximum of $50,000 of life insurance coverage. The employee can buy multiples of that. This has the advantage of group underwriting and lesser cost-per-person to install and maintain. So health problems that may be a personal obstacle to individual insurance are not necessarily an impediment when the insurance company is underwriting a group. The cost of placing the insurance may be lower because one group contract is created rather than many individual contracts.

And people do die. We experienced the death of one of our associates a couple of years ago. He was very well liked and is a much-missed member of our team. As hard as his death was to endure, it would have been even harder if we had not provided life insurance coverage. Although he had no dependents, and he died relatively young, the insurance proceeds allowed his mother to handle his financial obligations and final arrangements.

DISABILITY INSURANCE

The chance of becoming disabled at any age during a working career is higher than the chance of dying. That is true for the business owner too. Accidents, stroke, heart attack, and all of the maladies with which we are so familiar may interrupt or end a career. Disability is the largest cause of home foreclosures. And this risk can be mitigated, as group disability policies are not cost prohibitive.

Here is a special note for partnerships and personal service corporations with more than one shareholder. What happens when one partner or shareholder dies or becomes disabled? The remaining owner has to work twice as hard to run the business while buying out the interest of the deceased or incapacitated partner/owner. Life and disability insurance becomes an invaluable advance planning tool. Consult your attorney, accountant, and financial advisor for the correct configuration and cost structure for your business's protection.

Health Insurance

Most businesses require employees to contribute to their health insurance premiums and that is commonly accepted. In the author's opinion, no business should exist without providing adequate health insurance coverage to its employees, and the group contract should include major medical expense coverage. It is a competitive area, and most insurers offer multiple layers of coverage so that you will typically find a wide choice of contracts available. You can often obtain coverage as a small business through your industry associations or through business associations in your region.

I could not look into the eyes of my employees or their children if I did not provide health insurance coverage. Thus, I will be so bold as to urge you to shop for the contract that suits your pocketbook and employee makeup and counsel you to not begin business without this benefit in place.

Vacation, Sick, and Personal Days

This facet of your benefit package is both necessary and productivity enhancing. Vacations allow for domestic maintenance and for us to recharge our energy batteries, and personal days allow for necessary medical, legal, and tax-related activities. And if an employee is truly sick, you will not want them to infect the rest of your office or operation.

Once again, staying open to the good ideas generated within your company will save time, effort, and money. Debbie Sales, our managing director of operations, suggested the idea of "bucket days." We had been requiring individuals to specify the reason for taking a personal day or the reason for a sick day. If it was a personal day, it needed to conform to our accepted list of reasons for doing so. For example, it should be legal, medical, or children's school related. We still tell the story of an employee years ago who wanted, but was not granted, a personal day to change the snow tires on his automobile. If it was a sick day, we needed to know why and then decided if that was a sufficient level of sickness to justify a day off. Debbie raised the heretical thought of not requiring a reason and letting employees decide if they had a valid reason for taking the day off. Of course, my reaction was that the conscientious employee would properly use the opportunity, and the laggard would take advantage. Debbie patiently pointed out to me that this was already happening because people could lie to conform to our accepted list of justifiable activities or illnesses. So she reasoned, why were we forcing people to lie if they really wanted a day off and then burdening ourselves with the record keeping and verification duties? We added an incentive to not simply blow off the available days by allowing unused sick and personal days to morph into vacation days the following year in keeping with a conversion formula. Finally, we instituted a cash payment for unused sick, personal, and vacation days at normal retirement age. We do not mind financially rewarding long-time and productive employees who did not drag down our firm's productivity by using all of their sick and personal days throughout their careers. Conscientious employees have then, in effect, a deferred compensation plan in addition to their retirement plan. The laggard was going to lie anyhow, the honest person is rewarded, and we were freed from a frustrating and time-consuming task.

Cafeteria and Pretax Plans

With a reasonable amount of legal and accounting work, you can provide your employees and yourself with flexibility and tax savings. For example, public transportation, parking expense, and nonreimbursed medical expense can be handled through this type of plan. This section is not a recommendation to do anything but consult with your attorney and accountant on this subject. Each company's situation is different, and tax laws change with swirling regularity. But once aware of these opportunities, you can explore further.

Employee Education and Skills Training

Most small businesses cannot afford to and probably should not pay for advanced college degrees. We are entrepreneurs and should employ associates with an entrepreneurial and self-help mentality. However, job skills' training immediately benefits the company and should be encouraged and supported at every opportunity. Strategic partners and product providers can often provide this at little or no cost. Other professionals in the community will welcome the chance to instruct your associates. We regularly have attorneys and accountants, for example, teach continuing education to our people. Those professionals offer this for the same reason that you will want to teach at workplaces in your community.

Wellness and Self-Improvement Training

Your employees represent you to the public, and you depend on their energy and continued good health to drive your business forward. Having employees dressing well, quitting smoking, and losing unhealthful pounds are all beneficial for your business. Once again, this can be accomplished with little or no cost. Even when there is cost, an incentive program can turn the expense to your benefit. For example, we have had few smokers as employees over the years. But when we do, we offer to split the cost of a quit smoking program with them. If they remain nonsmokers for a year, we will reimburse the remaining half to them. That is a worthwhile investment in their productivity in the future and, frankly, their own self-esteem. If they are healthier and think well of themselves, they will be better employees.

FRINGE BENEFITS SUMMARY

Four important points are to be made concerning all of these fringe benefit offerings. First, you do not have to fully fund these benefits. You can partially fund them or not fund them at all. But you must make all appropriate benefits available to your employees. To not do so sends the message that your employees are not important to the company's success. If you inadvertently or consciously deliver that message to them, they will act accordingly toward you and your company's clients or customers thus undermining your efforts and chance of success. Most employees are conditioned to contribute partially toward the cost of their fringe benefits. View what is standard in your industry and do not fall below that sharing arrangement. This is not an expense. It is an investment in your most productive asset—people.

Second, you must educate your employees about these benefits. They should understand how to use the benefits package wisely or you will have spent your money with diminished return. Once they and their family members are educated as to how they can best use what you have provided, they will become appropriately appreciative. If they are not, you have either failed to properly communicate the benefits' value, or your hiring practices are not as effective as you might wish. Not everyone is an ideal candidate to work at your company. Hire only those who have the attitude that accentuates your vision and mission.

Third, fringe benefits do not always have to be costly. Rewarding the employee of the month, chosen on predetermined and objective criteria, with the parking space closest to the building is a no cost way to recognize and reward. Having monthly lunch and learn speakers on wellness, personal financial management, dressing for success, or interpersonal relations costs little or nothing. But providing these valued benefits helps to bind employees and their families to your company and boost productivity. An employee who is not distracted by financial problems works more efficiently and is less prone to agitate for higher compensation. An employee who has stopped smoking cigarettes statistically will take fewer days from work because of illness. An employee who dresses better and is in better physical condition will represent you more professionally.

Fourth, treat your employees as responsible adults. People will live up or down to expectations.

MANAGING WORKFORCE GROWTH

A final note on staffing and compensation covers growth in your workforce. Your people are your most valuable resource. Studies have shown that technical tools and resources are a secondary cause of success after the quality of your workforce. A terrific book on the management of teams and companies is *Corps Business* by David H. Freedman. Do not be put off if you are not military minded and do not assume stereotypes relative to military management. Give the book a try, and you will probably find it useful in formulating your own management style and communications structure. Build your team well, and it will serve your business.

An appreciation of your employees' value should not lull you into growing your workforce indiscriminately. Hire the right people and only the ones you need. Before enlarging your employee base, evaluate how increased productivity tools can boost efficiency. Talk with your existing employees and solicit their opinions about what you can do to help increase their efficiency. They know that you have only so much money to spend on payroll and equipment. If you enlist them as partners in helping shape your decisions, you likely will be rewarded with sound advice. When a company brings in management consultants, the soliciting of employees' good ideas should be their first action if they know their business. A lot of good thinking is bouncing off your walls every day. Make sure that you are harvesting it. Only after exploring productivity tools, strategic partnerships, part time assistance, and outsourcing should you judiciously add another team member and incur the concomitant expense of training, equipping, mentoring, and compensating that person. Business is about surviving and thriving. You cannot do either when you indiscriminately add overhead.

CHAPTER FIVE

LEAVING YOUR CURRENT EMPLOYER

PREPARING FOR THE D-DAY INVASION

Your structure, personnel, and resources are all planned. Now you must organize the actual steps you will take in moving to independence. Planning to leave your current employer to open your own business is a major undertaking, akin to planning the D-Day Invasion of Europe in World War II by the United States and its allies. Exaggeration? Not according to those of us who have done it. In most personal services practices, and in many other types of businesses, the employer feels that the clients or customers belong to the firm and, of course, the departing practitioner feels otherwise. A good deciding point is to evaluate who brought the client to the firm. In our company, our clients come to us via our educational seminars that are created, implemented, and paid for by the company's seminar and marketing department. As a result, clients come to our firm and not to individual financial consultants. The other way that we gain new clients is through referrals from our existing clients and through an organized networking effort with other professionals in the area. We naturally feel that our clients are the firm's clients. By contrast, a rathskeller model as is the case with many investment or real estate brokerage firms, does little to attract clients to their associates. Individual brokers must go out and establish relationships to build their own client bases, and oftentimes completely at their own expense. That seems to be a clear way of divining to whom the clients ethically belong. Beyond that, many firms require noncompete or nonsolicit agreements when taking on employees and associates. And that presents a stumbling point—surmountable or not—in moving clients or customers with you. Well-conceived and professionally written agreements often hold up. But even if they are not challenge proof, legal action to subvert them costs money and time. Sometimes the legal proceedings can place client contact in temporary limbo for both sides in the dispute.

The first step in planning your move is to decide who ethically owns the clients. Then determine if you can legally approach them relative to your move. You certainly will need a lawyer's advice if nonsolicit or noncompete agreements exist. Many lawyers will advise that a noncompete agreement is hard to enforce. However, it can be enforceable under certain geographic or time limitations. Nonsolicitation agreements are often more readily enforceable, especially for definable periods of time that may be extended for unique circumstantial reasons.

You can readily translate that acquired legal knowledge and experience to your new business when you fashion appropriate agreements for your employees to sign to protect your valuable business clients, their confidential data, and your proprietary processes and trade secrets.

At this point, you can begin planning for the move to independence. Some of the areas that you must evaluate and plan for in detail include the following:

- You need to decide where to house your business. The next chapter covers this.

- Your computer hardware and software requirements and other office equipment has to be planned in minute detail because you will not have time to make it up as you go during and after D-Day. This is also covered in a later chapter.

- A written timeline for everything has to be established. There is too much at stake to risk being disorganized.

- You need to decide how and when to include current staff in your project planning if you intend on taking some of them with you.

- The proper secrecy procedures must be employed to ensure a smooth transition.

Our own company story may be the best way to illustrate all of this. Our company began in 1972 as the author's individual practice in the investment business housed within an established investment brokerage firm. Over time, the business evolved as a result of the deregulation of commissions and the breaking down of the walls among the various facets of what has now become the financial services industry. Investments, insurance, commodities, banking, and cash management are now parts of one industry when they represented several distinct industries then. As my business grew, I added assistants in the James Bond, secret agent model. After 20 years in the business, my client base had grown to what was then considered to be the top tier of assets and revenues. But by the early 1990s, the industry had responded in true Darwinian fashion to the reduced revenues caused by the increased competition brought after the fall of fixed commissions.

A large portion of the brokerage industry responded to the decreased revenues spawned by deregulation by placing a heavy emphasis on internally manufactured investment and insurance products. This provided those firms with the profits associated with manufacturing products along with transactional commissions. This was not the result of bad people doing nefarious things. Rather, it represented a potentially viable response to change. By this point in time, I had a team of eight financial consultants, financial planning analysts, and administrative support people assisting me with my client work, all at my own expense. So, I had, if you will, an intrepreneurship rather than entrepreneurship. My host brokerage firm and I shared the revenues and the expenses in what was a rough parity. However, I supplied the clients from my seminar and referral gaining efforts. Life was comfortable, and there was no driving force to move to total independence. I knew that I could probably keep 20 cents more of each gross revenue dollar if I moved to total independence. But making more money was not enough of a factor to drive me to action as long as I was allowed to run my practice in keeping with my own vision, and I controlled my own revenues and expenses. Then, in 1994, another large company bought my parent firm. One giant swallowed another. Management changed and so did management philosophy. Heavy emphasis was placed on marketing internally generated proprietary products that were much more profitable for the firm. In fairness, they were committed to quality in their product manufacturing. But no one purveyor of investment products can have all the products that an investor will need. We believed we worked for the client and not the product manufacturer. Also, the new company attempted to shift the expense burden more heavily to us. Loss of control and pressure on profitability form a deadly combination. When that is coupled, as sometimes happens, with a lessening of respect for the individual professional and his or her efforts, it can lead to a parting of the ways as it did for my group from our host company.

This story will likely resonate with many readers as they may identify it with themselves and their current situations. That is why it is being told. But reacting to this type of circumstance from anger or without adequate analysis can spell disaster, as we will see as the story goes on. Fortunately, my group and I did not react hastily. But other individuals within the same national firm did with serious consequences.

By the summer of 1994, it was clear that we needed to move our group and our business to total independence. How we approached this is offered here as a template for each of you who may wish to make a similar move. I designated the year of 1995 to accomplishing key initiatives that would enable us to move with maximum client retention and minimal downtime without revenues. Remember that they were our clients as we created them solely from our own efforts. As a point of reference for readers, I will mention that I turned 50 in 1995 and was financially comfortable. The easy decision would have been to spend another five or ten years in the previous configuration and retire comfortably. But as has been discussed throughout this book, seeking independence is not solely about money. It just would not have been the right thing to do for our clients or for my own self-respect and self-actualization. So the planning began.

The following were the key independence initiatives:

- Upgrade our computer hardware from a support level of sophistication to where we could run an independent firm with the new configuration.
- Acquire the software necessary to run the firm independently.
- Identify a clearing broker/dealer firm as our strategic partner for back office work, which would be much more economical than to create such a resource solely for our firm.
- Locate and build out the office space that we would need.

All of that occurred according to plan because we had a plan. Without one, we would have consistently had to make it up as we went along. An undertaking as large and critical to you as your own business cannot be accomplished haphazardly. A myriad of details needed to be coordinated over the year of planning. You will not necessarily need a year, but you will need the organizational structure and planning.

PROTECTING YOUR CONFIDENTIALITY

As we moved through the various arrangements with each potential landlord, real estate agent, and equipment supplier, we had each sign a statement of acknowledgment that what we were discussing must be held in the strictest of confidence. By their signature, they verified that they understood they could be held legally and financially responsible for any breach of that confidence, which served as a big deterrent to gossip. Not one of our potential business liaisons breached our confidence.

The investment industry is like many others. Once an employer or sponsoring company becomes aware of a pending move, it usually will lock out the associate. The host firm retains files, databases, and notes. Although no one likes the secrecy, it is necessary to protect your valuable business assets prior to moving to your own business. The secrecy and sometimes even subterfuge, but never illegality, is likened to the actions surrounding World War II's D-Day Invasion of Europe.

An example of inadequate secrecy will illustrate the danger. Another financial advisor was planning to leave the same firm for the same reasons one month after we did. He was located in another city, and we were not associated in any way in business. Because we were further along than he in our preparations, he would call us for advice. I cautioned him as to the required secrecy, but he felt that the branch manager where he was housed would not betray him because he had served as a groomsman in the advisor's wedding, and they had been close friends for years. I tried to get him to understand the risk he would take in sharing his plans with his manager/friend. He divulged his plans one Friday evening after work over a sociable cocktail. When he arrived for work the following Monday morning, he was locked out without files or other data. He was relegated to calling his clients sitting on the carpet of his yet-to-be-furnished new office using a cell phone, as the landlines had not yet been installed. This was not the professional posture that he wished to present to his clients, and he was at a distinct disadvantage to the brokers at his former office who were enticing his clients to stay at the old firm with the full benefit of all of his notes and records.

A move to independence must be planned and implemented with the same degree of secrecy that a life or death struggle would entail. And it is life or death, at least from a financial perspective. For most of us, such secrecy and even subterfuge seems distasteful. All such plans should be made with appropriate legal advice so as to not unwittingly stray over the line to illegality and to fully protect your own business interests. But within the parameters of the law, you must do all that you can to protect yourself, your family, and your associates in your new venture from the potential of predatory practices of your soon-to-be-former firm.

Another story continues the illustration. A friend left his financial services firm to move to another. He resigned and spent the afternoon going about the large office shaking hands and saying good-by to his former colleagues. As he left each office, those people began calling his accounts that had been reassigned to them by the office manager. By the time he got to his new office, all of his clients had been called and enticed with special offers to remain with the former firm. Remember that he created those accounts, not his former firm. It is a war, and you must steel your mind to that bloodless, but potentially costly competition.

A date for departure should be picked for maximum benefit to you. That should occur at a time when your potential adversaries for the retention of the clients are away or at least present in lesser numbers. We selected the latter part of the Friday afternoon prior to the three day President's Day weekend. Yet we still had brokers trying to raid our accounts calling them over the weekend. At least there were fewer attempting to do so than would otherwise have been the case.

Finally, do not take whatever happens personally. It is, as the movie said, "just business." Everyone looks out for his or her own interests, and those will not coincide with yours. Your previous firm feels that the clients belong to it just as you feel the opposite. The former associates from your newly departed rathskeller feel it's their duty to keep your clients. You will waste valuable energy being resentful over their actions and will inadvertently transmit that negativity to your clients as you discuss their following you to your new business. Everyone loses as a result. So, take the high road. Once it is all over, you can always follow up on patently illegal or unethical action on the part of your adversaries. But stay unruffled in the heat of the battle.

CHAPTER SIX

CHOOSING YOUR BUSINESS SPACE

You will have so many expenses in beginning your own business that you may be tempted to save money with cheaper office space and furnishings. You might rationalize this by vowing to upgrade once the revenues start rolling in on a regular basis. Don't do it! You are judged by your office, your automobile, how you dress, and a lot more. That is not an argument for buying the most expensive or the most exclusive designer goods. Rather, it is a dictate to use appropriate marketing tools and avoid diminishing your perceived competence and worth in the eyes of clients and prospects. You should not take office or business space in declining neighborhoods. You should locate where other successful businesses are located. In most cities, that is the central business district or an upscale suburban office park. If you locate your personal service business, for example, above a strip shopping mall along a suburban road, you always will be thought of a second-best to the competitor who was willing to invest properly in his or her business.

INTERIOR DESIGN

The clients who select you will reflect your economic positioning. An old maxim is worth remembering. You will be as wealthy as your clients. This is not an argument for elitism. Rather, it is a prescription for inclusiveness. Envision your ideal client and structure your office to serve that client. Everyone else will also identify with you as they see themselves as equally deserving of competent professional assistance. You do not need gold-plated bathroom faucets. But you do need to look like the competent professional that you are. Leverage your skills and knowledge with an interior designer. This person specializes in areas where you likely have little expertise. Ideally, use a designer who does not represent the furniture manufacturer, but who works for you on a fee basis. A simple example followed by a functional example will help solidify this suggestion.

The simple example was our designer's suggestion that we deviate from the building standard of vertically slatted draw blinds for our front conference room that is visible from the atrium in our building. My reaction was a busy, "What's the difference?" She took me to another floor and showed me the difference. When the wide, vertical blinds are drawn back, they give the appearance of a storeroom. Our horizontally slatted blinds look good closed or drawn, even nine years later. Small point? No it's not. People draw conclusions on visuals, sometimes without even realizing that they are.

The functional example is that of our kitchen. I asked for a kitchen and also a group meeting room. This would be in addition to client conference rooms. Our designer suggested a combined kitchen and group meeting room. That has paid dividends ever since. It has become the clubhouse and meeting place for good ideas and interaction. Visit our offices in the early morning, and you will find our people buttering their toast and collaborating on the day's projects and activities. Many impromptu meetings occur there throughout the day. It is handy, and people go there for refreshments and naturally talk about common projects. It is a comfortable space to collaborate. We also host many charity board and committee meetings in our office and have a large and well-appointed training room for doing so. Once a committee meets in our offices, we usually hear a request to use the kitchen for meetings because it's so "homey," and they can get to the coffee, soft drinks, and fridge easily. If people feel that comfortable with you and your offices, they become more than business acquaintances. Use a skilled, experienced and nonbiased interior designer to plan your office space who knows how things are supposed to flow.

OFFICE LOCATION AND IMAGE

Your physical positioning of your office in the community should reflect the geographic diversification of your client or customer base. You must be more concerned with the convenience of your customers in getting to your office than your proximity to your home or favorite recreational activities. You should dress in a way that reflects how you wish your clients to see you and not for your personal comfort. Your choice of a haircut and personal accessories should inspire trust and not the preferences of spouse or friends.

Harsh? Phony? Not at all. People deal with those who inspire trust and confidence. If you wish to be successful, you need to engender those feelings in others with your competence, integrity, and presentation of yourself and your business. It must pervade everything from your shoes to your business literature and stationery. To do less gives your competitors an advantage they do not deserve.

Office or business space does not have to be the most expensive in town (in fact, it should not be because it could spur thoughts of your pricing being too high). You should be located in class A or A- or, at worst, B+ space. An older, well-kept building of historic significance can be even more impressive than a newer, more expensive structure. Look for who else is housed there. Are they businesses and professionals with whom you would seek to associate? This is a good indicator because you will be judged by those companies surrounding you. Weave a story about your building that catches your clients' imagination and associates you with a quality of the building. In our case, we chose a restored building first constructed in 1929—the year of the Great Stock Market Crash. We tour prospective clients through our space and relate the enduring qualities of solid building construction with that of solid investment portfolio construction. Good quality methods, materials, and workmanship endure through all time periods and business cycles where cheaper, quicker methods must be torn down and redone.

We also relay a self-deprecating story about the great bargain we obtained in our long-term rental rates. To take the edge off a seeming boast, we explain that our search for economical, but good quality space brought us to the previous building owners who were anxious to rent the vacant space prior to putting the building on the market. We contrast that to the much more expensive space across the street that rented for full current pricing. In describing our good fortune in gaining an economical, long-term lease, we connect it to a client benefit. If we are judicious in our business cost structure, we should not have to seek fee price increases simply to cover our poor business judgment or extravagance. It is worth the time to tell the story because clients always react well to it. Clients will understand and appreciate that the judicious judgment of their attorney, accountant, financial advisor, architect, or medical service professional is working on their behalf as well.

FINDING THE RIGHT BUILDING

First, find the general location that you desire. If it is in the central business district, decide what portions of that downtown area suit you. List the buildings in that area where you would feel comfortable. This next step is important. Walk around that area and imagine yourself as a client coming to visit you. What do you see as you enter those prospective office or business locations? Is the lobby or entry area clean? Are the door frames, baseboards, and other trim free of nicks and dings? Or does the entry look tired? How do building personnel treat you as a visitor? That is how they will greet your clients or customers. We took such a walking tour years back and found a distinct difference in how we were treated among the various buildings that we thought were good office space opportunities. Our choice based on this observation has been borne out over the years as our clients and our employees continue to be treated with respect and helpfulness. Our building's personnel and building services, such as cafeteria and barbershop, tend to reflect the attitude of our building's management under the guidance of the very capable Wayne Rodgers and Judy Carmichael. We have found the same family-like atmosphere when requesting routine maintenance, negotiating upgrades, and renewing our lease. By contrast, we regularly hear complaints from business acquaintances who are housed in the buildings we rejected because of poor treatment during our exploratory walking tour. All of this becomes part of your image that is projected to your clients and prospects as they visit you. Make it the best image that you can through advance scrutiny.

NEGOTIATING FOR SPACE

Hire a tenant representative. It will not cost you anymore than you are going to spend anyhow, and will likely save you money. At the least, you will gain more in amenities or benefits for the same money. The tenant representative is your personal realtor. Most buildings have a certain amount of realtor's commission built into the rent for showing and negotiating the space that you will take. If you deal directly with the building owner's realty representative, he or she gets all of that commission. If you use a tenant representative, that same commission is shared between the two representatives. So, use that money to gain expertise on your side.

Your business may be like mine where I occasionally meet do-it-yourself folks who think they are smarter than the professional. They are not, because they do not have the education, experience, tools, and knowledge of the marketplace that the professional possesses. That's true in real estate also. You can benefit from all of that by hiring a knowledgeable professional to put all of that to work for you. Also, don't be overly concerned about conflicts of interest. Most realtors in town, like most attorneys, know each other but are honest professionals when they represent their clients. In our case, we settled on the building we wanted, and our tenant rep (the very competent and dedicated Peter Hackney who died tragically too young soon after) began negotiating with the building's rep. By coincidence, the same large commercial realty firm employed them both, but that was not a problem. They negotiated so hard that they, at one point, were shouting and waving their arms at each other.

The same relationship and payment method exists for the architect who will design your space if it needs building out or remodeling for your occupancy. That cost is built into the rent. If the building's architect does the work, he or she will represent the owner in every recommendation and decision. If the cost and the work are shared with your architect, your interests are represented too.

But even with the utilization of knowledgeable professionals, you still must have knowledge of the negotiating process so that you can make informed judgments. Although the professional does a lot of the work, you still must make the critical judgments that will impact your business for years to come. This is analogous to trusting my physician to advise and treat me appropriately, but when the big decisions are presented regarding treatment alternatives, I can feel confident in making those that are best for me if I am properly informed.

The following paragraphs outline some of the moving parts of a building lease transaction. Other parts of the country and other building owners may present their transaction somewhat differently, but they all will follow generally agreed on building owners' standards.

Your rent will be quoted on a cost per square foot, annualized basis, such as $20 or $30. When they give you a dollar number, it always should mean per year, per square foot of space. This is the first major variable.

The second variable is your share of common space. This refers to your allocation of the building lobby, your hallways, the rest rooms, and the like. It is expressed as an added percentage of your space, for example, 10 percent or 15 percent. This is more of a pricing issue than an actual calculation of the common space you will use. A 15 percent common space allocation means that you will spend 5 percent more in total annual rent than if your allocation were 10 percent. Here is where your tenant rep will be of great value. He or she knows what fair pricing should be and should not let you assume a higher percentage than necessary to complete a competitive deal.

A utilities and property tax escalation clause is standard. It is fair to the owner and allows the owner to give you a competitive rent price from the onset of your lease without having to build in unknown contingencies for future possible increases. This way you are only paying for real increases in the future. It is standard for your first full year to form a base year and increases should begin after that. Be sure to negotiate a full year at least before allowing an escalator clause to take effect. We once had a lease presented to us on a satellite office location beginning mid-year with the escalator clause becoming effective the following January. We rejected that, and the owner revised the agreement to have us sign the lease. If we had not been alert or had been shy about pursuing our interests, we would have overpaid unnecessarily.

If your space needs remodeling or building out for you, that cost will be reflected in the rental price you are quoted. Generally, the longer the lease you sign, the more competitive the pricing because the owner can amortize the cost of the remodeling over a longer rental income stream period. A good tenant, offering dependable revenue over a long period of time, will induce the owner to absorb more of the construction cost than a shorter-term lease. We just had our offices recarpeted by our building at no cost to us simply for adding two years on to our lease—for the same rental cost we had been paying. Sensible owners like good long-term tenants. Being a responsible businessperson as well as a responsible tenant usually pays tangible dividends.

Most long-term leases contain rent escalator clauses. This is different from utility and tax escalators and again will be expressed in dollar terms as is price per square foot per year. Prices of most things do go up over time. As long as the price increase amounts are reasonable and competitive, you should have no fear of this. But with good negotiating skills and alertness, you can negate an escalator rent number that later becomes unfavorable. During the economic recession of 2000 through 2002, we approached our building owner a year prior to our lease expiration. Our rent had risen per the escalator clause written into our 1995 lease. The building offered us a lower rent for extending early and we accepted—but only if they lowered our rent to that number right away. They were happy to do so and retain a good paying tenant who continues to bring quality clients to the building on a daily basis, some of whom may be also looking for space. And we got complete recarpeting as mentioned earlier for adding two years to the lease beyond that at the same low rental pricing. The point here is not negotiating skill. Rather, it is knowing what is competitively possible in the current economic climate and getting the right professional advice to reasonably pursue your interests. Everybody wins as a result, the landlord included.

You may be asked to provide a letter of credit covering the lease payments as a new business owner, and we will discuss that in the financing chapter.

A last word on office or business space: you will need more than you initially think, so that you will want to contract for a little bit more than you feel you will use. It will fill up sooner than you expect assuming a successful launch of your business. Also, part of your lease negotiation should be to identify growth space in the building, ideally contiguous to your contracted space. This expressed desire will not hurt your negotiating posture either. Don't spend any money to hold potential space in your building. Your building owner should simply promise you in a letter that you have first right of refusal on the identified potential future growth space.

CHAPTER SEVEN

EQUIPMENT AND SUPPLIES

THE RUBBER BAND PHENOMENON

Remember to arrange for your start-up equipment and initial ordering of supplies using the confidentiality agreement described in Chapter 6. The copy machine salesperson who talks to an office mate who wishes to make points with your current employer may cause you to sit on a carpet calling your clients on a cell phone. This will not be nearly as impressive to your clients than if you were to do the same from a desk, with proper telephone gear, with all of your client files, and with secretarial assistance.

Also, be aware that most banks readily will make equipment loans collateralized solely by that equipment provided you carry a good credit history. And many equipment manufacturers and distributors have purchase or lease arrangements available. It is advisable to spread your equipment costs over several years so as to preserve your capital for payroll and client project expense. Generally, you will want to buy the most serviceable equipment available and not the cheapest. But you likely will not need the most expensive either. Like real estate, your equipment should reflect your desired image. A home-quality telephone voice message system will not project the professional environment and competence that inspires customer trust. The correct equipment and systems should also pay for themselves in reduced labor costs over time. Talk in those terms to the equipment suppliers and challenge them to justify the purchase based on functionality in your business along with time and labor savings. For example, a letter-folding machine will pay for itself in labor cost almost immediately if you regularly send general client letters or advisories.

Consider equipment-servicing contracts. Although it may seem initially costly, the chief advantage is having a technician on immediate call rather than trying to find one at a crucial time in a client proposal, a trial, or at the height of the tax-filing season.

Supplies are different. Order all that you need but only that. Pricing varies, and the marketplace is competitive. Most suppliers deliver, even the big discount chains. Don't tie up capital and floor space storing future supplies.

When we contracted for our initial order of office supplies, someone misread the quantity denomination, and we bought enough rubber bands to supply us for years. So, after donating several cartons of rubber bands to Animal Friends, Pittsburgh's no-kill animal shelter, we still had enough rubber bands left to supply us until the remainder became so brittle and dry that they had to be thrown out. Fortunately, they were inexpensive and provided a cheap lesson in just-in-time supplies purchasing. You do not want to run out of, say, copy machine paper. Yet, you do not want to store more than a month's supply when the provider will deliver regularly. You may want to establish a relationship with a service-oriented supplier whose prices are competitive. Then have your administrative personnel periodically check competitive prices. That service-oriented supplier will likely meet or come close to meeting the competitive prices to keep your business, and be appreciative of the opportunity to remain your supplier. Do not assume efficient pricing on the part of your suppliers. Help keep them up to date with your administrative person's vigilance.

CHAPTER EIGHT

FINANCING

In addition to equipment financing, you may need a line of credit or other loans. As we learned, lack of adequate seed capital is a prime reason for business failure, and so is too much debt. Do not go into business for yourself if you are undercapitalized. Correspondingly, you do not need, and probably should not have, an abundance of capital. Under-capitalization causes failure, and over-capitalization causes complacency. You should feel the pressure to be efficient and to work hard. But you should not have to sweat every payroll period. The following paragraphs outline what you need.

Begin with a solid pro forma profit and loss statement prepared using your industry knowledge and the professional expertise of your accountant.

It is important to have sufficient capital on hand to get you comfortably into the period when your pro forma shows that sufficient business revenues will be available to carry the business on a month to month basis.

Make sure you have proper equipment financing or capital to purchase all of the business tools and systems that you will need to get started and maintain your business. You should not count on future revenues to buy needed equipment. The equipment loan repayments should program comfortably into your pro forma.

A line of credit at your bank to cover timing differences between receipt of planned revenues and expenses is important. The bank will want a personal guarantee by you of the line's repayment even if you are incorporated. This is normal and should not be construed as the bank's commentary on your business's success potential. They will naturally try to cover their exposure. If you believe in yourself and your ability to succeed, this is a normal rite of passage into entrepreneurship. However, they may also ask to collateralize the line of credit by filing a lien on your house. This is usually unnecessary unless the line you are seeking is overly large. Then you may want to recalculate your true need. But if you are asking for a reasonably sized line of credit, and your accountant concurs, keep shopping for a competitive offer from another bank. Usually your own bank knows you, will be the setting for your first conversation, and will offer a successful conclusion. (Remember your confidentiality agreement.) If they are not accommodating, rely on the free and open competitive capitalist system to locate a new bank that values your business. Not all banks see the small businessperson as their desired customer. Find one that does and create a potentially long-term relationship that will serve you both well through the years.

Your landlord may ask for a letter of credit from a bank to cover the lease repayments. This is normal for a new business owner even if your personal credit history is positive. If your personal credit is poor, the landlord usually will not offer a lease to you under any circumstances. The letter of credit is requested because, although you have dutifully paid your mortgage and charge card balances, you haven't incurred this level of credit before. The building owner may ask for a letter of credit to cover the entire length of the lease, and you will counter, through your tenant rep, that you will obtain the letter for only the first year or, at most, two. You will pay the bank a fee each year for providing the letter, so a shorter period will save you money. Your rationale to the owner is that a year or two is sufficient for you to establish a good pay history, and you are not obligated to indemnify the owner for all future business risk. Your rep will point out to the landlord that it is unlikely that all of the other business tenants have provided a full lease letter of credit. The landlord will usually agree, as the initial length requested was just a bargaining position. But you might be surprised how many tenants go for it when not properly advised by a professional.

It bears reemphasizing the importance of enlisting your accountant and spending adequate time in preparing a viable pro forma revenue and expense statement. This exercise will point you to the right
level of debt and the proper repayment terms and will assist the bank
and your landlord in making favorable business judgments about
you.

CHAPTER NINE

LEGAL FORMAT AND PROTECTING YOUR INVESTMENT

INCORPORATE OR NOT?

You will want to protect yourself and your business from liability and loss. This can be done through the legal format you choose for your business and with insurance protection. No defense is absolute, but these will be your primary lines of defense. In addition, the choice of legal format will impact the ongoing taxes that you and your business will pay. Your attorney should be consulted for advice on both topics, and this book cannot substitute for that. The following information is provided to help prepare you to approach the subject with a general understanding.

Forms of business ownership fall into three categories. The first is sole proprietorship. This is the most common form of small business ownership. The shoemaker or the management consultant works under his or her own name and is not incorporated. The individual's credit and the business's credit are one and the same because the individual is the business entity. The liability of the business is the same as for the individual. There is no corporate veil of liability protection because there is no corporation.

The second form of business ownership is partnership. This follows the same format as a sole proprietorship, but two or more individuals own the business as partners. The credit and liability profiles are the same, but are shared among the partners jointly and severally.

The third type of business ownership is a corporation. This is an entity unto itself. It is incorporated under the laws of a state, and those laws govern its operation. It stands on its own credit, if it can, and attracts liability to itself rather than its owners. But under certain circumstances, the credit of the corporation is insufficient and the owner or owners have to back up that credit with a personal guarantee. Also, under some conditions, the liability claim may pierce the corporate veil and flow through to the owners. This could occur under several sets of circumstances, but primarily would occur when owners or officers act fraudulently or when the business of the corporation is made up totally of the owner's personal expertise. A surgeon or a financial advisor cannot effectively claim the corporation was at fault if malpractice occurs. For the personal service provider, the act of incorporating does not remove the corporation's owner from the credit or liability arenas. The decision to incorporate usually has more to do with tax planning.

The following lists three different types of corporations:

- C corporations are taxed as a separate entity. This allows for some judgments to be made and timing differences used in planning for the tax recognition of profits.

- S corporations recognize all profits and losses as accruing to the owners instead of the corporation. This eliminates the potential for double taxation at the corporate and then the individual level.

- Limited Liability Company (LLC) is a hybrid structure that includes the liability protection of a corporation, such as that may be, together with the flexibility of a partnership.

The proper business structure choice is not a do-it-yourself project. It requires legal guidance. You can prep yourself for that discussion by viewing the excellent summary contained in the U.S. Small Business Administration web site. The business structure discussion is housed at the time of this writing at www.sbs.gov/starting_business/legal/forms.html.

Let your attorney be your expert guide. Discuss your vision for the future of your business with your accountant and your attorney, ideally in concert with the creation of the pro forma profit and loss statement that you a creating with your accountant's help. These professionals can properly guide you in the choice of a legal format, but only after they understand how you see your business evolving.

PROTECTING YOUR BUSINESS INVESTMENT

As a personal service provider, you expect to deliver competent advice and guidance to your clients and customers. But sometimes you make mistakes that can only be rectified at some cost. And we all realize that people do not have to be in the right to bring a suit against you. It would be imprudent for you to assume full financial liability in such cases, and that's why you must obtain malpractice or errors and omissions insurance. You can often find appropriate coverage through professional or business associations as well as through strategic partners. For example, the realtors' or architects' association or your clearing broker/dealer can usually negotiate a complete and cost effective contract that you cannot obtain as advantageously by yourself. Sometimes a government body or agency can help as is the case now in some states where medical malpractice insurance is in jeopardy. The premium cost is usually lowered with the use of a deductible, often $5,000 or $10,000. Read the contract closely to identify exceptions. Regardless of cost, you must have it. The risk is too great to omit this coverage.

The same is true of property and casualty insurance. The risk because of loss of your valuable business property or liability because of bodily injury or property damage to others caused by your business activity is far greater than the modest cost of coverage. Obtain your insurance from an agency that is experienced with business insurance. If you employ contractors on your premises, ask for printed evidence of their workers compensation and liability insurance coverage. If they do not provide coverage for their workers, the liability may fall to you.

Be sure to comply with all state regulations governing workers' compensation insurance and do not ever compensate employees other than in a legal manner. The small savings to be had by saving a Social Security payment or other insurance premium will be quickly and resoundingly offset by the potential legal and financial repercussions in being found out. Why state the obvious with such conviction? We do because employers routinely flout the rules without sufficient forethought and at great peril.

Your employees may present a liability to you if you use improper or poorly constructed personnel policies. We created what is commonly called a personnel manual. But we title it our *Guidelines for Association.* It embodies the ideas and prohibitions one would normally consider for a personnel guidebook, but also includes a codification of our culture. You will want to do the same and be sure that you have your manual or guidelines reviewed by a labor attorney. Choose someone who has experience defending employers against employee claims. An experienced labor attorney will know what to say and how. Consider the legal fee as a one-time insurance premium against employer liability. And don't be afraid to take action in the case of violations. Seemingly innocent actions can put you at risk. Recently, a purveyor visited our office to deliver products. One of the deliverymen evidently thought one of our firm's young women to be attractive and commented so. At his request, the purveyor later called our office to inquire about her. Innocent? Likely so. Not worth my attention? Dead wrong! I immediately queried the young woman to find if she felt threatened by the incident or if anything untoward was said. All was fine on that score. Next, our administrative manager called the purveyor and explained that we do not allow that type of action on our premises. Why become involved? Because to not do so could have left us open to a charge of permitting a hostile or harassing work environment. I got personally involved in discussing the incident with the employee because I wanted to send a clear signal that any potentially harassing action by anyone was considered serious. Most importantly, I have an obligation to my employees in today's world of wanton violent action to place their safety first. You cannot just put it in your manual. You have to also be ready to act on your rules and beliefs.

◆

CHAPTER TEN

ASK WHAT YOUR GOVERNMENT CAN DO FOR YOU

FEDERAL GOVERNMENT

At the federal level, the most visible and ready assistance comes from the U.S. Small Business Administration (SBA). This agency provides classroom training, printed literature, and mentoring programs for small businesses in addition to loans. Their web site is www.sba.gov. The following list includes some of the highlights of their offerings relative to starting your own business:

- Starting your business
- Financing your business
- Managing your business
- Business opportunities
- Disaster recovery

In addition, the SBA provides an extensive online library of more than 200 hundred free publications on business startup and management along with connections to business news, magazines, and resource links. The SBA maintains a small-business training network and provides information on laws and regulations. It also provides guidance on doing business with the U.S. government.

When the SBA provides assistance with financing, it does so with commercial lending partners, so that the same criteria will apply if you apply for loans on your own. The SBA will help guide you through the process and will become a meaningful conduit to financing. Because government programs change with regularity, it serves no purpose to detail current offerings. The SBA web site will provide the most current information available.

Finally, the SBA also administers the SCORE program. This is the Service Core of Retired Executives who volunteer their time to counsel small business owners on topics covering both specialized and general business management.

STATE GOVERNMENT

The programs offered by the 50 state governments vary. As an example, Pennsylvania's web site (www.state.pa.us) offers information on the following topics:

- Starting a business
- Economic development
- Expanding a business
- Doing business with the Commonwealth of Pennsylvania
- Government services
- Finding employees
- Maintaining a business
- Licenses and licensing
- Minority- and women-owned businesses
- Workers compensation issues

Under the section "Starting a Business," information is available on financial and technical assistance, site finding, and "The Entrepreneur's Guide—Starting and Growing a Business in Pennsylvania" in printable format.

LOCAL GOVERNMENT

Likely, your local municipal government will also provide assistance. In Pittsburgh and its surrounding Allegheny County, the primary assistance is available through the Urban Redevelopment Authority (URA), which assists businesses to locate within the county and the City of Pittsburgh.

OTHER NOT-FOR-PROFIT RESOURCES

Other public, but nongovernmental, resources might include entrepreneurial centers at local universities or colleges. Pittsburgh has two, at Duquesne University and at the University of Pittsburgh.

Here is the stated mission of the assistance center at Duquesne University (from the university web site at www.duq.edu/sbdc) quoted as typical of the type of help often available through your local college or university:

> The Duquesne University Chrysler Corporation Small Business Development Center (SBDC) is a member of a statewide consortium of college and university-based centers designed to provide comprehensive management and technical assistance to the small business community in Pennsylvania. The program is jointly funded by the U.S. Small Business Administration, Pennsylvania Department of Community and Economic Development and public and private agencies.
>
> The Duquesne University Chrysler Corporation SBDC offers both one-to-one and team consulting to identify and address the problems of small business clients. The SBDC consultants provide management consulting tailored to fit

the needs of small business clients in Southwestern Pennsylvania. In addition to General Management consulting, both International and Environmental consulting are available.

Your local library can be a wonderful resource online using their web site and in person with the aid of knowledgeable research personnel. The Carnegie Library of Pittsburgh is an example. Their web site guides a reader easily to the business library's section. There the small business resources become immediately apparent and include business plan preparation and index, web site connections for small businesses, and demographic information. The small business resources sector lists assistance on business and market information, taxes, export assistance, minority and women's business, legal and accounting issues, and entrepreneurship. The entrepreneurship tab lists a host of governmental and nonprofit assistance for small business start-ups. The business library holds weekly lectures on topics of general business interest and of importance to small business owners.

All of these governmental, educationally based, and research-oriented resources are available to you without charge or at a reasonable cost. You are well advised to consult them during the planning phase of your move to independence.

CHAPTER ELEVEN

CONVERTING EXISTING CLIENTS OR CUSTOMERS TO YOUR NEW BUSINESS

We previously covered the need for confidentiality and even secrecy in planning your move to independence. The necessary self-protective steps, likened to the preparation for surprise required for World War II's D-Day Invasion, are not exaggerated in preparing for your physical move and new business housing arrangements. And that certainly extends to your relationships with your existing customers or clients leading up to and through your move to your own business. As was discussed previously, you must decide if your existing clients are ethically yours and when you can legally contact them. The ethical part refers to how they were acquired. Did those clients come to you through the efforts and expense of your current employer? Did you do anything to gain and retain them beyond accepting the accounts and servicing them? Those are the questions, but the answers are unique to you and your situation. If after honest and fair evaluation, you feel those clients are yours because you brought them to the firm, and they stayed at the firm primarily because of you and not just because you want to take them, then you can proceed on to the next question. Are they legally yours to contact? Your current firm may have legal prohibitions in place that is usually evidenced in the form of signed agreements and/or written company policies. Adherence to those policies would normally be a condition of your employment. Look for those agreements and written policies and take them to an experienced labor attorney for a professional opinion before taking action that may prove prejudicial and costly to your new enterprise.

A couple of examples will serve well here. A hair salon chain has employee policies that its employees sign on employment. The policy states that, on leaving for competing employment, departing employees cannot work within a certain geographic radius expressed in miles from the location where they were employed. The owner of the salon chain justifies this on the basis that salon patrons come to the business because of the international reputation of the owner and the very expensive and upscale advertising used to build the business. Departing employees who felt they could solicit their former clients found themselves defending a breach of contract suit in court. Better for them to have checked in advance as to the time and cost involved. Defending themselves, coupled with the poor public relations for their new business affiliation and former clients, made lack of attention to detail a major negative.

The next example is that of a financial advisor who left a large national firm and sought to take his clients with him. He had developed those clients and was solely responsible for servicing them. That covered the ethical consideration. But, although he was also a lawyer, he failed to anticipate and counter in advance the possibility of an injunction filed by his former employer. The firm injunctioned him, and he counter-injunctioned his former firm. At that point, neither party could talk to his clients, all of whom had assets invested with his former firm, and they could not gain advice from either party. That made for some very nervous clients and anxious moments for the advisor over a two-week period. It finally was legally resolved at some cost to the advisor in legal fees, and he began to repair his client relationships. The moral of the story is: do not neglect the ethical and, especially, the legal preparations. It does not have to be a nightmare, but it can be if there is lack of attention to detail and insufficient preparation.

Once you have thoroughly analyzed the ethical and legal considerations and feel you are both correct and safe to approach your current clients, you should plan your action steps. Not contacting your clients in advance of your move will make you very anxious as you would like to know if your revenue pro forma is accurate. However, you should not contact them. Expecting to move a certain percentage of clients and having the attendant revenues begin within a short period of time is understandably a big motivator in wanting to gain advance client agreement. But resist the urge! There are two valid reasons why you should not contact your clients in advance. First, they remain the clients of your current firm, and you may prejudice your legal standing by soliciting them to move while you are still employed there. The second reason not to contact them in advance is that one or more of your clients may feel sufficiently uncomfortable with your pending move to call your current employer to discuss it. You cannot have your clients sign a confidentiality agreement, and they legitimately may wish to explore options between going with you or staying with your current firm. It will only take one call to give you away and thwart your exit plan.

Plan your action steps and timetable in resigning and approaching those clients who are legitimately yours. And stick to your plan. We detailed the story earlier of a financial advisor who resigned and then took the time to say good-by to each of the other advisors in his rathskeller-structured office. As he left each advisor's office, they began calling his clients to induce them to stay. Also, as he had not been in the office for a week prior to resigning, and he had confided in some trusted "friends" in the office, he had clearly telegraphed his intent to leave. The branch manager had already predistributed his accounts to others so they could call his clients as soon as he had delivered his cordial good-byes. Cold? Hard? Yes, that is the world of many firms. You do not wish to be part of that, but you will be hurt by it if you do not consider your departing actions carefully in advance and work your action plan.

Your action steps to transition your clients in preparation for and during your move may include the following actions.

Gather the lists of your clients that you are legally allowed to compile. Compile or copy needed items from client or customer records and files that, once again, are legally permitted in the view of your attorney.

Premake all necessary transfer, new account, and authorization forms for client or customer signatures immediately on your resignation from your current employer. This is critical, as you will want your clients to receive transfer forms or letters in the morning mail following your resignation. It will be much safer if they have them to sign and return as you make your immediate follow-up call. Otherwise, you will allow time for your former employer to fashion special incentives for them to stay.

To help ensure that your mailing reaches your clients the morning after your resignation, become familiar with the mailing zones involved and have them bundled by zip code and mailed first class. Take the trouble to have your mailings delivered to the central mailing facility in your city. Immediate handling by the post office is critical. Do not use second class mail for such an important mailing to save a few dollars or trust the timing of mail pick up at the corner mailbox or branch post office.

Create an easily maintained database of completed necessary client actions, such as signed new account forms received back from clients, and so on, so that you are not wasting valuable client interface time with haphazard notes and redundant actions.

Create and maintain an up-to-date database of client contact information. You will not want to fumble with scraps of paper and telephone books at the time of your "invasion."

Make a schematic of how paperwork will be handled and who will process it along with built-in checkpoints for controlling its flow and completion. For a comprehensive view, make sure you enlist your team in this exercise and mentally and verbally rehearse the workflow. The D-Day invaders rehearsed for months to limit casualties and help ensure success. So must you, as your casualties would be financial losses and unrealized goals.

If you follow this plan, you will find yourself spending your "invasion" time doing what you should. And that is conversing with your clients or customers and making them comfortable with the benefits of following you to your new business. This is much more productive than shepherding ill-planned administrative details and uncoordinated support staff. With adequate secrecy and proper advance planning and practice drills, you will have completed your "invasion" before the "enemy" (those trying to take your hard-earned accounts) can mount an effective counterattack. A final note is to prepare your associates whom you have decided to take with you and your support staff. Preparation includes intensive conversation about adequate secrecy and training drills—offsite and not on your current employer's time—in preparation for the "invasion" day and afterward. It is better to be overly prepared than to be found wanting.

Another example illustrates the extent to which your business adversaries may go and the resulting need for planning. A financial advisor was moving to independence from a large national firm. Somehow his firm became suspicious (Loose lips sink ships!) and hired a private investigative firm to follow the advisor's secretary. (You may not like it, but it does get that nasty.) Because of prior planning and a quick phone call to her boss, the financial advisor, the secretary did not panic and had the presence of mind to go to the movies. His employer paid two private detectives to watch movies that afternoon with the advisor's secretary.

This stage of your transition, where you are talking with your clients or customers about moving with you to independence, will be enhanced by the work you have done on your value proposition. Your clients know how good a practitioner you are. That's why they are your clients. Your move to independence is the time to let them know how your value to them will increase with this move. In this way, you are not just asking them to move with you because you wish them to do so. They may do that, but you are giving them concrete reasons why they, their families, and their employees will be better off for moving with you. It would be a good idea to include a written statement of your value ladder proposition with the transfer forms. Make sure to get your attorney's approval on the wording you are using.

Your current clients or customers trust you with their business, their assets, and the success of their businesses and endeavors. You must justify that trust with adequate planning and with a flawless execution of your plan so that you can continue to serve them as an independent businessperson. In addition to keeping the trust and respect of your customers, you will be rewarded with the all-important revenues they will provide to you in those early and crucial months of your new business and for years to come. They are your clients to keep or to lose. Don't let the other side win them away.

CHAPTER TWELVE

GAINING NEW CLIENTS AND CUSTOMERS— THE RIGHT WAY

"MAN MUST SIT IN CHAIR WITH MOUTH OPEN FOR VERY LONG TIME BEFORE ROAST DUCK FLY IN."

Sometimes professionals feel they are, or their profession is, demeaned by marketing. They feel that clients will flock to them because their capabilities will be recognized. We would all like it to be that way. But the old fable was right. You cannot hide your light under a bushel and expect people to lift the bushel and discover it. You have to lift the bushel and show your light to people who may care. You must market yourself. That may take many forms, and we will discuss them in this chapter. But brilliant as you may be, you must first find people to be brilliant to. The old Chinese proverb is apt here, "Man must sit in chair for very long time with mouth open before roast duck fly in." So let's go hunting in a way that suits your talents and your profession.

Previously, we discussed ways of gaining new clients or customers as a part of determining your ideal business structure, and we examined the sales continuum. Now we will focus on these issues exclusively from the view of what works, why, and how to implement those initiatives.

The sales continuum reflects the entire process of finding people who will be interested in your services, good servicing after they become customers, and gaining new clients as referrals. It looks like this:

Leads→Prospects→Clients→Service→Referrals to new clients

It all starts with leads. No matter if you are an insurance professional, an attorney, or an investment banker. You must have people to whom you can describe your service and a way to identify and follow up on their interest in your service. That person is a lead.

There are several ways to gain leads, and we discussed earlier the view that cold calling is, well, cold and sometimes in conflict with the image you wish to present to prospects and to the community. Here are other ways to generate leads.

ADVERTISING

Advertising is expensive, and it does not work for some businesses or professions in generating leads. We have come to believe through experience that advertising is effective for financial firms like ours in creating awareness and even credibility. But it is an unreliable way to gain new clients. People do not tend to select investment advisors from advertising in sufficient numbers to justify the expense. This seems borne out by the scant calls or walk-ins experienced by the "broker-of-the-day" at the branch offices of national investment brokerage firms. And this is after the expenditure of millions of dollars for advertising. However, when an employee of such a firm gives a lecture or is referred by an existing client to a prospect, the advertising precedes the employee and helps pave the way with solid imagery and credibility. Most personal service providers are well advised to consider this and to tailor any advertising to creating a comfortable companion outreach to other business building initiatives.

Advertising alone usually will not build your business. But when you do advertise, direct it to segments of the marketplace where you wish to gain new clients who fit your business model. For example, we have many radio stations in Pittsburgh, and they are relatively well stratified as they likely are in your community. We could choose to advertise on an all-news station or on one that plays music and presents talk banter for older adults. Another available station has the widest geographic listening audience. A first thought would be to select the widest possible listening audience and concentrate all of our efforts there with potentially maximum listening. An evaluation and some judgment indicated to us that we would be paying far too much to reach many people who, by geography or income and asset demographics, would not be prospects for us. Also, although the other, older-listening audience station would seem to attract folks with more accumulated assets for potential investing, further analysis indicated they have high assets, but lower levels of income. So the assets were likely nonliquid and real estate oriented, namely their primary and resort homes. Finally, the all-news station when measured by assets, income, and employment position was our best value purchase even though it presented a smaller listening audience. Seems obvious? Well, not at first—until we poured through the data each station offered to support their position. The same reasoning and research pointed us to advertising in the weekly business newspaper, the *Pittsburgh Business Times* versus the larger local dailies.

Once the media is selected, the message must be framed for the desired audience. We wish to attract individuals who have investment assets and who are accomplished in their life's work. We accept other folks as clients, but do not wish to commit scarce corporate resources attracting anyone other than our ideal client. Our message is framed for individuals who are serious about the realization of their life's goals and have the assets and earning power to deploy an effective plan for reaching those goals. You too must craft your value proposition message to the profile of your desired client.

PUBLIC RELATIONS

Public relations (PR) is usually a very cost effective way of getting your name out to the community and helping to smooth the way to productive conversations with prospective clients and customers. You would be wise to seek PR opportunities that suit your value proposition and where the subject and message delivered are pointed toward the clients that you wish to attract. It can be counterproductive to appear in print talking about a segment of the marketplace that you wish to shun or answering a question that runs counter to your values. We know an advisor who wrote a book advising young couples on how to begin and implement financial planning and investments. She is now associated with counseling young folks with high aspirations and low assets. That was not the marketplace she courted, but she seems to have boxed herself into that corner with her topic choice. Another example is our oft-received request from business editors to pick the best stocks for the upcoming year or quarter. Our firm's philosophy is built on a platform of complete asset allocation and diversification for serious investors, not speculators in individual stocks. Succumbing to the allure to appear in print answering this question will only encourage hot stock pickers to contact us, and they are not our desired clients.

Ways to gain good PR include getting to know the business editor of your local daily newspaper or business weekly newspaper or radio or television program manager. You will become a regular for interviews and opinions on topics within your professional competence, but only if you demonstrate such competence. You will not be interviewed or quoted if you hound the editor for "ink" or airtime. He or she will avoid you and the negative image you represent. But if you are sincerely interested in your area of competence and care about seeing it well represented, that honest approach would be appreciated and used by the editor. The cornerstones of good PR are honesty and good judgment. And it doesn't hurt to have the skill of a good sound bite. Editors and reporters do not want to sort through an involved technical treatise. They have a deadline to meet and appreciate when you make it easier for them.

A recent example occurred with the business columnist of a local metropolitan daily. The columnist periodically calls for an opinion or quote. He calls many of the investment managers and advisors locally so as to gain the widest possible perspective for his readers. He wrote an article recently that lambasted a popular financial investment product used by many advisors. Some of his criticism was justified because some advisors may use this product in applications when it should not be used, much like an over-prescribed medication. But he misunderstood one feature of the product and erroneously reported his misunderstanding as a product flaw. Several financial professionals immediately e-mailed scathing rebukes. The columnist was trying to fairly present a problem in product application to his reading public and made a mistake. Our response was to e-mail praise for his attempt to educate the readers and to correct his misinterpretation. He telephoned as a result of the e-mail, and we discussed the product and its applications in detail. He then wrote a correction and guess who was prominently quoted in the article as having helped to set him straight? Not the guys who lambasted him. If you want to be quoted in your local or the national press, treat the editors and reporters the same way that you treat your best clients, with honesty, respect, and displayed competence in your professional or business field of expertise.

Your field of expertise will determine your method of approach to the media. Who writes about your industry and business? If you are a tax specialist, find who covers that topic at the local popular and business papers or on local radio or television. The same is true for legal, financial, architecture, or hair styling. They usually won't do lunch as they are not looking to be entertained, and attempts to do so may be viewed as unprofessional influencing. Rather, a straightforward e-mail, phone call, or letter will often establish the beginning of a solid communicating relationship. Send your contacts the information that you feel they would benefit from seeing, but don't overdo it. You can also send your opinions to your contacts, and that is even more valuable to them than a boring dissertation on technical matters. An example of this came from an exchange with my physician a few years ago at the onset of managed care. I likened what happened in medicine to the investment industry when it deregulated two decades earlier. The idea was presented to the editor of the local business weekly and resulted in an invitation to write a column on the subject.

All of the times that your clients, other referring professionals, and your prospects in the community see you being quoted in print, writing a column, or expressing an expert opinion amount to tremendous credibility for you when they come into contact with you through your other marketing efforts.

CREATE YOUR OWN PUBLIC RELATIONS THROUGH NEWSLETTERS AND E-NEWSLETTERS

Sending hard copy newsletters and e-news is an excellent way to inform your clients and to stay on the minds of prospects. It will also generate leads. We have received calls from nonclients on our newsletter list asking to meet with one of our advisors and citing our newsletters. The common phrase we hear is that our newsletter advised and guided them more regularly and aptly than their current advisors who were being paid to do that. That brings us to a key in creating good PR via newsletters—do not buy canned newsletters. They appear to be what they are and feel very impersonal for your clients and prospects. If you are going to the expense of creating this medium of communication, take the extra time to make it reflect your value proposition and attempt to connect the reader to your organization with stories and articles of interest written by your people, complete with photographs. It should not be slick, but it should look professional. And most of all, it should be informative and sincere. Every article should inform, but in a way that embodies your firm's values and your unique way of implementing those values. It is important to distinguish that you will not promote your firm. Rather, you will promote your firm's way of assisting clients. Once you have written the first newsletter, the subsequent issues will be much easier.

This will be true of e-newsletters also, which will be single page items with a more timely feel to them. Recipients of the e-news should feel that it is of immediate import and that they can absorb it quickly. Some folks eschew hard copy totally in favor of electronic news. We believe there are two problems with that. The first is the obvious one that not every client is electronically connected or savvy. Second, e-news has a few seconds of potential life where the recipient decides to read it, save it for later reading, or, in many cases, delete it. By contrast, the hard copy newsletter stays in the reading stack and also has a potential secondary and tertiary readership as the original recipients send it to friends, family, or business associates when they deem that an article seems helpful to others.

We do a hard copy, multipage newsletter on the calendar quarters and an e-newsletter in the other eight months. The hard copy news always carries a block requesting up-to-date e-mail addresses so that the reader can receive our e-news in intervening months. It works, period. We get many compliments from clients, referring professionals, and prospects. And that is not because we rival the *Economist* in content. Rather, we hear comments like, "Your article on education funding was short, complete and to the point. I sent it on to my son." That is your purpose in sending a newsletter for your business or practice. If you own a restaurant, don't simply send out a tabulation of dining specials. Include articles on intelligent dining or how to spot fresh ingredients in a prepared meal. Your knowledge and articulation of those topics implies your value proposition for your customers. If you are an accountant, don't simply regurgitate this year's tax laws. Create an article listing the 10 worst mistakes that individuals make in tax preparation. In spotting themselves in your list, you make the reader value what you offer based on your demonstrated knowledge. Think about it. As an experienced restaurateur or accountant, you can write the article quickly based solely on your expertise.

Our newsletters are meant to make what we do real for clients and others. So should yours. We are not threatening to unseat Ernest Hemingway's reputation here, just to communicate what we know and practice everyday.

Writing these articles is not a chore. Our ad agency, Krakoff Communications, handles the layout design and the mechanics of printing and distribution. Although recommended, using an ad agency is not strictly necessary for you. You can enlist a freelancer experienced in newsletter design and production or even a college intern from the local journalism school to oversee the actual compilation and printing. And you will use a mail house to fold and mail your newsletters. The total cost will be reasonable, and you will have gained targeted and meaningful public relations exposure.

We use a batch e-mail processing company for our e-newsletters. The Karol Company in Pittsburgh very economically provides this service to us. We thusly overcome the problem of spam e-mail screening, and we do not have our personnel tied up for a day trying to send our e-mails. See Appendix B for examples of both our newsletter and our e-news.

You can also write columns and articles for local newspapers and magazines. The opportunities surround you. View every suburban weekly newspaper and local magazine. Every one of them looks for interesting and timely articles to include in their publications. Approach the editors directly and ask if they have need for your expertise in their publication. They may ask you to advertise, but most professional editors will not make this a requirement. They simply want good copy that will interest their readers. Here are two examples of such columns. One was written for *Primo,* a national affinity group publication for Italian-Americans (Figure 12.1). The second was printed in the Allegheny County Medical Society's quarterly bulletin, which is sent to all physicians and other medical providers in our area (Figure 12.2).

DIRECT MAIL

Direct mail can be an effective method for gaining leads that may be turned into prospects for your services. However, blanket direct mail campaigns to addresses without prequalification of the resident or business is very costly and often ineffective. You should have some concept of the person or entity to which you are mailing to create a reasonable cost-per-lead generated. Some examples would include obtaining the list of retirement plans in your marketing area so that you are mailing only to those business that may have an interest in

road to success | ROBERT FRAGASSO

My parents have worked hard all their lives in their small business. I'm concerned that they may lose everything in retirement if one of them should require nursing home care. What can be done to prevent this?

Brian Grilli
LaVale, Maryland

Brian, people like your parents who have worked hard to accumulate assets, bear the greatest risk. Those without assets are covered by government assistance provided by your state's Department of Welfare called Medicaid. The wealthy can pay without depleting their children's inheritance and bankrupting themselves. But, your parents may be forced to spend down their savings because they are neither rich nor poor.

Nursing home and home health care expenditures fall into two categories. First is skilled nursing home care that may be needed for rehabilitation after a hospital stay. Medicare, which is the federal government's health insurance for retired people, pays for this.

The next level is long term care. This means the patient is cared for at home, and is called home health care or they receive care in a nursing home. Private and government health insurance does not cover long-term care expenses. The cost of this is about $5000 per month, or $60,000 per year. The average nursing home stay is three years, and with nursing home cost inflation of 5% that totals $190,000 for a three-year stay. Personal assets must cover this. But if the patient and spouse are without assets, Medicaid (different from Medicare) will pay. Medicaid payments come from general taxes, so we all participate in paying those costs for folks who cannot pay. When people hide or give away their assets to family members prior to entering a nursing home, they are placing the burden for their support on everyone else. The federal and state governments have severe penalties for attempting this and for any advisors who counsel you to do so in contravention of the law. But Brian, there is a two-step solution that your parents should consider. First, have an analysis done to see if their assets will be sufficient to

cover one spouse in a nursing home and still support the other spouse at home. This kind of analysis is not burdensome or expensive and can be done for you by a competent financial planner or accountant.

If the assets prove insufficient, or if your parents do not want their life's savings going to a nursing home, they should purchase nursing home and home health care insurance. This can be bought at any age, but people should evaluate this by age 60. The chances of needing nursing or home health care double with each decade of life. The premiums usually stay level for life once you have a contract. Shop carefully as this is a major purchase that you will want to keep in force. Deal with only established insurance companies and knowledgeable agents.

If any of our readers have questions on this or other financial planning or investment subjects, email Bob at robert_fragasso@fragassogroup.com .All questions are answered. The Fragasso Group, Inc., headquartered in Pittsburgh, PA, is a Registered Investment Advisor and counsels individuals and corporations. Visit its web site at www.fragassogroup.com.

Figure 12.1   Road to Success

Retirement Planning and the Real World

ROBERT FRAGASSO

Medical doctors are retiring. For most of the more than three decades that I have been in professional practice that was not the case. But, given today's economic and litigious climate, physicians are not only retiring, they are often opting for an early retirement. This gives rise to problems that did not previously require attention and addressing. You will need a nest egg upon which to retire comfortably and to enable the pursuit of avocations that will replace medical practice. Those can include charitable work, business activities, family, fitness, travel or a less demanding but lower paying career. Whatever is in your future, you must be financially prepared, and today is the first day of the rest of your life.

So, you are thinking ahead to retirement and wondering if you will be able to financially handle it. How can you be sure? You don't want to run out of money or use up your assets. That's a common concern and the best way we know to answer it is with the facts as they are currently known. You must scrutinize three areas closely so that you can make good decisions and then move confidently into that great retirement adventure.

First, do a retirement capital projection. That is a schedule where you project your expenses for the first year of retirement and then grow them at the expected rate of inflation. Expenses include everything from

monthly needs to the annual items such as insurance premiums and taxes. Where expenses are not fixed, such as a life insurance premium, you must grow that first year's number using a historically realistic inflation number. Throw in the one-time expected expenses roughly when you think they'll occur, such as a wedding or gifts to grandchildren for education expense. Once your expenses are identified, take expected income such as Social Security and pension benefits and apply them to those needs. The shortfall must be made up from your investment assets and savings. So, you will then take your assets and grow them at the total rate of return you are currently positioned to expect. For example, if all in bonds, use a bond rate of return. If in a balanced portfolio, use a balanced return that is supported by a longer-term track record. The past is no guarantee of the future, but a longer-term track record is the best reference point in this exercise. If the projection shows you running out of money before you're actually expected to run out of breath, you need to adjust your assumptions. Maybe you can't retire right now. Or, maybe you have to spend less or increase your expected return on investments with a better portfolio allocation in order to reach your goals. You should enlist your financial planner to help you with this process. He or she has the software to run the

Figure 12.2 Retirement Planning and the Real World

your retirement plan investment management services. Another might be to obtain a list of luxury item purchasers if you plan to offer your upscale and expensive hairstyling or day spa services. It makes no sense to mail to every household in an area when many are scraping together the money for a cut-rate haircut. Search for proclivity indicators to your type and level of service. This becomes somewhat easier where there are enclaves of higher priced homes or an expensive office building setting. Yet, that may not always be the case. An expensive home may not be the best indicator of ability to invest in securities, for example. The home owners may still be saving up for furniture to fill their empty living and dining rooms before being able to invest to prefund their children's education expense or their retirement security. As much as is possible, try to identify indicators that the direct mail recipient is able and willing to consider your services. Mailing fewer to better prospects may gain a better net return than mailing more to the masses.

List brokers can be helpful in targeting a more productive mailing. But you can also do this with the aid of your public library's resources and even using the telephone book. We created much of our targeted database in the early years by using the business telephone book (called the yellow pages back then) to develop our database of named professionals in the community. Every attorney, accountant, physician, dentist, chiropractor, architect, consulting engineer, and others who could be identified by individual name was inputted into our computerized database. Don't mail to businesses without an individual's name or at least a title, such as "Retirement Plan Trustee" to better ensure a viewing of your material. You can also compile a list of every officer of publicly held companies in a geographic area by requesting annual reports for those companies. Many can be viewed online. All of a company's officers are listed in that report, and the mailing address is that of the company. Even governmental bodies can provide low- or no-cost lists. Here are two examples. First, most municipalities have plot plan maps for every residence. The names of owners are not shown, but the addresses are. So, if you wished to mail to every resident in a particularly desirable residential community, your personnel or college intern could input every desired address and title them "Home Owner" or "Resident."

The second example involves the federal government's Freedom of Information Act. Some years ago, I wished to have a list of the retirement plans in our geographic area as that is a primary market for us in managing investment assets. We wished to mail information to the trustees that would be of timely interest. The list brokers had that data available, but at a price that we did not feel we wished to pay. So a call to the Department of Labor in Washington, D.C., provided the insight that the desired data would be available from the federal government at an extremely reasonable cost. You can get what you need to develop your business if you are creative and tenacious enough.

Do not hesitate to call federal, state, or local agencies seeking information. Most are willing to assist, and most data are available by law.

Depending on the type of service and professional constraints of your industry, direct mail can work in either or both of two ways.

DIRECT MAIL TIED TO DEMONSTRATION OR CONSULTATION

The first involves a direct mail program that invites a prospect to visit your location for a consultation, screening, or initial trial of your service. This can be used when the canons of your profession prohibit direct solicitations, as may be the case with medical providers or attorneys, but allow for the offering of a screening or consulting appointment. It can be especially effective when the screening or initial consultation is the best way to demonstrate your service. Examples could be a medical screening of prostate-specific antigen (PSA) levels or blood pressure by a medical service provider, a consulting appointment with a chiropractor, an evaluation by a nutritional counselor, or it could be a complimentary portfolio review by an investment professional or a scrutiny of tax returns by a tax accountant for deductions missed. This is a fair way to identify leads, as the individuals who will contact you are those who believe they may need or benefit from your service, and it allows you to suggest remedies that may be provided as a part of your ongoing service. This is definitely preferable to service providers who phone people from a list hoping to find someone who may wish to talk with them.

It is not necessary, and is even advisable, to follow the herd when considering a direct mail or other marketing initiative. You probably have not seen it, but consider the possible beneficial outcomes to a residential architect who mails an engaging, benefits-laden capabilities brochure to the residents of an affluent neighborhood of older, stately homes. A professional and sincere cover letter points out the benefits to the homeowners when consulting with an architect before engaging in a remodeling project and describes how true value may be added to their homes by integrating modern amenities with historic architectural design. The cost of the mailing is modest, and only one response turning into a commission to provide design would turn a profit. And best of all, the architect is spending time talking only with legitimate and interested leads.

DIRECT MAIL OFFERING INFORMATION ON RESPONSE

This can be especially effective because it gives the service provider a higher degree of control in the response sequence. It works like this.

A compelling, professional letter is sent to a list of likely candidates for the provider's service. It may include a brochure, but it certainly would include a response card and postage-paid return envelope. Recipients can request information on a topic of compelling interest. This must be of readily apparent benefit to the recipients to receive this information, and returning the card will bring that information to them. It should be made clear that there is no cost or any obligation in requesting the information. The response card will contain spaces to furnish all appropriate contact information.

Once the response is received, and the requested information is sent, the service provider should call to *arrange an appointment,* not to answer questions on the phone. The phone call references the information requested and delivers an initial and general benefits statement. Then the service provider should request a 20-minute appointment to briefly and professionally discuss needs and how the service will address those needs. No games, pretenses, or showy salesmanship.

A professional is responding to a request for information that was sent, and the fact of the request itself signified a potential need. The chief tool here is respectful and friendly, but incisive, questions. If an appointment cannot be arranged, ask for permission to keep them on your regular newsletter list, which we discussed previously. There is a reason why they requested your offered information, and it wasn't because the prospect needed fireplace starter material. The better you become at helpful and straightforward questioning and conversation, the more introductory appointments you will arrange.

Confirm the introductory meeting the day prior. Where possible, have your support person do this for you to avoid getting into a question and answer discussion prematurely.

Begin the meeting the next day by repeating the benefits statement that caused you to gain the appointment. This is important as most people have not memorized your prior conversation, and many other personal and business concerns have come before them since you spoke by phone. Once you have stated a clear and concise benefit, end with a open ended question—one that cannot be answered by a simple yes or no. And please remember not to answer your own question. Let your prospect do that no matter how long it takes. Do not fear dead airtime. He or she will eventually answer in some fashion. When the answer comes, you have a conversation. This is far different from delivering a sales pitch to a stone-faced listener and hoping that you may have said something intriguing. Once you have learned what is important to this person, you have license to explain what you do and how it will address his or her need—but never before that. And do not describe every benefit and feature of your product at this point. Talk about only those that pertain to the needs the prospect articulated. You will have plenty of opportunity to list all of the other features of your service before this transaction is completed. For now, you are trying to move that person from lead to prospect. Focusing on what is important to him or her is the way to do it.

Many times, professionals are reluctant to follow these instructions because they feel they have something of value, and the prospect should immediately recognize this. You wish that were true, but it often is not. Try this and you will find a whole new world of prospect and client communication open for you.

End the meeting committing to a concrete next step. That may be a visit to your office, a data gathering appointment, or whatever is the next action step in your process. A subset may be to arrange an interim half step, and that is fine. But without a concrete course of action begun, you do not have a prospect. A legitimate prospect appreciates a meaningful movement toward his or her goal. A casual listener who does not intend to move forward at this time will not allow the process to progress.

Remember that these are people who are potentially interested in your service, or they would not have arranged the appointment. So many of the introductory meetings will result in new clients. Even if they do not immediately become clients, they may in the future, and they may refer you to others even right after the introductory meeting.

This methodology of direct mail offering information on response works. It is a numbers exercise. A certain percentage of the recipients will request information, and a percentage of those will make an appointment with you. A percentage of those will become clients and/or refer you to others. Some of the variables that determine those percentages are outlined in the following paragraphs.

The quality of the households or businesses to which you first mail your introductory letter and materials is very important. Homework time spent gaining likely lists will pay off in higher response rates.

An example goes back to the author's early years in building his business. I needed to create a mailing list for an offer of information regarding saving taxes through one's investment portfolio. After determining my audience would be those in apparently higher tax brackets, simply looking in the yellow pages for professionals (in potentially higher tax brackets) listed by individual name furnished a productive mailing list. A high school or college intern can input all of the physicians, dentists, allied medical service practitioners, attorneys, accountants, architects, and consulting engineers from the directory into a mailing database. Most of the professionals who became clients 30 years ago from this methodology are clients today. They and the author are older and grayer, but nonetheless mutually grateful for the long term and beneficial business and personal relationship.

Your proficiency in conversing with prospective clients will result in more and more productive appointments. Invest in yourself with a Dale Carnegie sales course or hire an accomplished sales coach. Our firm has used both. The local Dale Carnegie organization, owned by

Peter and Gerri Graziotto, has trained many of our people. Also, John Rosso, owner of Peak Performance Management in Pittsburgh, has provided customized training for our associates. Remember that you are not "selling" people. You are learning to uncover their needs so as to help them. You must learn to get past your own mental clutter so you can do this efficiently and effectively. That is what this training teaches. All of that results in you getting to practice your profession to assist many more appreciative clients than otherwise and to make a better living for yourself and your family.

Another variable is the level of efficient organization within your operation. You should not do the routine work of data entry, initial mailing, or response mailing. You must touch only your highest and best uses in this process. That includes only conceptualizing your message, guiding the mailings to the best possible recipients, and conversing with prospective clients. Others should handle all of the rest of the process. Even if you do not currently have a staff, this can be economically delegated to your children, interns, or a stay-at-home person looking for extra money. Today's world of personal computers and off-the-shelf databases make this much easier than my 30-year-ago mailings that required a completely manual process. Now, the entire exercise is handled by one of our people during a minority portion of the workweek and then sent to a mail house for economical and labor-saving handling.

NETWORKING: THE NATURAL WAY TO GAIN NEW CLIENTS

WHY NETWORKING?

It compliments all other business-getting efforts. Advertising, public relations, and even lectures and seminars precondition the public to know who you are. It is easy because it is part of your daily life and activities. It opens you up to new people, experiences, and ideas. Being nice to people is fun and just a better way to live.

What Is Networking?

It is simply being aware of and interacting with the people you come into contact with in all of your activities. It can also include the creation of new opportunities to meet people with whom you can interact.

Where Are Some of the Places Where You Can Network?

The short answer is "Everywhere!" The following paragraphs list some categories for interacting.

Business life.   This would be with every one you meet in business including clients, purveyors, other professionals, and even competitors. Our competitors have complimented us to others. This doesn't happen by accident.

Social life.   Friends, neighbors, and fellow religious or social organization members should all become aware of what you do for a living and how helpful you, your company, and your methodology are for people seeking your services.

Everyday activities.   This means being alert to opportunities to talk to people, not about what you do, but about themselves as you go about the daily activities of transportation, shopping, restaurant visits, children's activities, and even dog walking.

How to Network?

It's simple and step-oriented.

First, *you must be pleasant and outgoing. You must be correctly perceived as approachable.* Find opportunities to talk with people about what relates to them or what is going on around you. You will be amazed how people will open up about themselves when you speak to them in a pleasant and interesting way. Here is a real-life example. The author was standing in a concession line at Pittsburgh's Kennywood amusement park near a pregnant woman and her family. (While waiting, why not be pleasant?) The initial comment went something like, "Well, I guess you won't be riding the roller coasters today," with a pleasant smile. Want to guess how quickly we discussed the whole story of the pregnancy, how many children they have, where they are living, and why they need to buy a new home? Pretty quickly is the answer. You can usually learn everything about someone in 5 to 10 minutes of casual conversation when you ask a question or make a cordial comment and are sincerely interested in the response you get.

Second, *regardless of how you start the conversation, if you are genuinely interested in other people, they usually feel socially compelled to ask you about yourself at some point.* This is your opportunity to deliver *short and meaningful* answers to their questions. Do not give them your entire history and philosophy on life. They're not really interested in that much detail. What you say should have universal application and not be narrowly focused on you. An example question to you might be "What do you do for a living?" A wrong answer would be, "I manage portfolios and spend lots of my time researching investments and getting financial consultants ready for their client meetings." (Please wake me when this is over!) A better answer would be, "I manage portfolios for individuals and retirement plans." What happens next? They either ask other questions like, "Where do you work? And "What's a good stock to buy?" Or they'll say something like, "I never do well with investments." Any of those questions or comments invites you to elaborate or to ask more questions of your own. It's not a sales pitch, but a conversation.

Third, *the conversation may be helped a bit if you're wearing logo clothing for your business.* Our trademarked logo is a distinctive light house shown at night, surrounded by dangerous rocks and a stormy sea and the companion phrase, "We Guide, You Decide." No one needs a lighthouse near a calm harbor on a sunny day, which is usually where you see a lighthouse logo (see Figure 12.3). People do ask about it, and that jump-starts the conversation.

Figure 12.3   Trade-marked Logo

The best way to network is to be in proximity to the kind of people with whom you want to interact. Participating in or joining activities or organizations where achieving people or those with potential need for your services congregate is very helpful. The following are some examples of some potentially productive arenas and organizations:

- Professional groups
- Chambers of commerce
- Professional or industry societies
- Networking clubs
- Book clubs
- Bowling leagues
- Golf, athletic, or country clubs
- Travel groups
- Affinity interest or background groups
- Children's sports or play organizations
- Avocation or charitable activities
- Religious organizations
- Fund-raising activities
- Boards and committees
- Political organizations and initiatives

You are on display and being scrutinized in all of your outside activities, whether you realize it or even like it. Why not make it the most fun that you can by interacting sociably and productively with your fellow participants and life travelers? But remember that you have no license to talk about your work or your firm unless asked by other people. You can cause that to happen by being approachable and by asking them about themselves. One of the best ways to generate interest in you and your business is *by being the most competent and most sincere person you can possibly be concerning the activities you are engaged in outside of the office.* People will be impressed with your honesty, sincerity, and skills, and they will naturally gravitate toward you. It is natural for people who are impressed with your competence, good judgment, and approachability as a board member or children's sports coach to assume you carry over those qualities into your professional life. They will select themselves to you.

Here is a note of caution. Do not become involved in activities solely for business-getting opportunities. No matter how you try to hide that, people will discern the insincerity. Be involved with the charities and organizations that you truly care about. Your zeal and good performance there will be the best attraction of new business, and you will not have to think about it or work at it—provided that you have mastered your value proposition until it becomes second nature for the time when people do approach you.

EDUCATIONAL SEMINARS

This is the single best way to gain new clients whether you are a new business or one that has been established for years. Established businesses must constantly gain new clients or customers also. People die, move, businesses merge, and, occasionally, a client or customer is captured by a competitor. Not working to add new clients or customers dooms a business to regress. For a start-up business, it is imperative to put new business acquisition at the fore. Educational seminars will bring clients to you. Why? There are several compelling factors with this initiative.

First, seminar attendees self-select topics of interest and, usually, of immediate import to them. If they selected your seminar, they probably are shopping for the kind of help that you can provide. People do not attend, for example, a seminar on estate planning as entertainment or take their time for one on maintaining a healthy back if they are not experiencing back ailments. They need professional assistance, or at least good information on the subject.

Second, attendees have the opportunity to observe the instructor and evaluate his or her professional views and methods. Although you will *not* talk about yourself and your firm in this seminar, the essence of you will still come through. That will be true both professionally and personally. People want to deal with folks they trust. Observing you over a period of, say, three evenings at an adult educational course will create a bond and a trust that is real. You will always be their "professor" even years after they have become clients, and their children have grown and become clients.

Third, the people who are not compatible for your personal service will not select themselves to you as clients. And you will not want them as clients as they will clog your system and bog down your efforts to be efficient. A good example from our seminars that we still do today after 33 years in business is our debunking of stock market timing. We do not believe this can be done and attempts to time markets cause unnecessary risk. We teach our belief in the folly of attempts at market timing in our courses and give hard statistical data to support our position. As a result, we do not attract clients who expect us to time markets. This means we do not set them and us up for a failed relationship, and we do not waste time with recalcitrant clients who would drain time and energy from properly servicing our methodology-compatible clients.

Fourth, part of the experience of the educational seminar should be to have the attendees compile their data relative to the topic area and then have created an analysis of where they stand relative to the goals they have articulated for themselves. The discrepancy between where they wish to go and where they are headed will be stark in many cases, and they will conclude that they need professional help to right the course. You, as the instructor who have inspired them and helped them to identify this, will be the likely professional for them to ask for that assistance. The key is that they must complete a data form. Short of that, you will receive accolades, but few new clients from your efforts. Also, the completion of the data form is a clear signal that they are serious about addressing their problem. Lots of folks are willing to talk and never take action. Resolve is signaled by the action of compiling the information required to begin your process. It is presented as a part of the class work, and the noncommercial nature of the exercise is stressed. We give the attendees a sample of the analysis they will receive as a result of their homework assignment. This takes away the mystery and concern and replaces it with the desire for what they see and its benefits.

We do a dinner certificate raffle at the last class, and the raffle ticket is the completed data form. It comes across tastefully because we explain that the class will be beneficial only if they turn the material into a concrete and actionable plan for reaching their life's financial goals. Absent that, they have simply gained unused information. We illustrate the noncommercial nature of the plan process and then explain that the data can be submitted after the class has concluded, regardless of time elapsed. We go on to describe how our late submission record grew from 2 years to 10 and then 14 years after class. People laugh and get the idea as we pose the dinner certificate raffle as a way to encourage them to do what is beneficial to them in a timely manner.

The sponsored, educational seminar contrasts sharply to the dinner seminar at a club or hotel that is often seen advertised. The reader of the ad is fairly certain that they will be sold a product or service at the dinner seminar. But even if you do a dinner-type affair, and we would recommend that you do so only for established clients and their invited guests, you must make it an educational experience, not a sales pitch. A truly educational experience is your best sales pitch. You are showing prospective clients how your thinking and methods can solve problems. But you cannot demonstrate that until you have allowed prospects to see that they have a problem and how it will adversely impact their goals. In our experience, that is why the multisession, educational, nondinner seminar works best.

Go to our web site, www.fragassogroup.com, to see how we present our seminars, for whom, and what materials we use. It will help you embark on your educational outreach marketing. The topic of properly given educational seminars requires a book of its own. In summary, the methodology includes the following components and steps.

GAIN AN EDUCATIONAL SPONSOR

An educational sponsor may be a college, university, or community college. Find one that has an already established adult educational curriculum. In that way, you will benefit from the dissemination of the institution's course catalog that will include your course. You may do supplemental promotion in the form of a flyer advertising your course and its benefits to attendees. Get it out to everyone in your sphere of influence in the most economical way possible. Be creative and a little gutsy. Why not? Who else is going to service clients better in your field than you? Lift the bushel and show your light! Get your health club to allow flyers to be put in the inevitable display rack that also holds flyers on upcoming 5K races and the like. Put an advertisement in your church or other organization's bulletin. ("My that nice Ms. So and So is giving a lecture at the college. I got to know and like her after she asked about my garden at the last committee meeting.") It does not have to be held at the college. A library or community center sponsor can be just as valuable. But you have to be able to demonstrate that your talk will be 100 percent educational and not pitch products or services. Be very direct with the sponsor that you do this because you like to teach, and it keeps you current with developments in your field. But you also do it because some of the attendees may decide you can help them. You will leave that to them and will not solicit business. Your direct honesty will be appreciated and understood. The college, library, and community center have to attract customers and patrons too, and your ancillary promotion will help them. The facility or program director knows how this process works. And if you discover that one does not, that wasn't the right venue for you, and you are better served to find another.

An example from some years ago may bring this into focus. I was asked to address a retired persons' group. But the program chairman admonished me that I could bring no literature about my company or even mention my role or where I work. Naturally my answer to him was a question: "Please give me one reason why I would wish to address your group in light of the restrictions you have just placed on me?" He stopped and began to smile. He explained that he was sensitized to a previous financial services provider who came to talk and used the entire time to speak about himself and his company. I then explained how we deliver our educational lectures and what attendees gain from them. He gave me the go ahead to mention my company name and have literature available for taking on a voluntary basis. You can usually resolve most such issues with a clear statement of your value proposition regarding every aspect of your business ready to deliver as needed. By the way, we retain today valued clients who selected themselves to us after that talk.

GAIN A CORPORATE SPONSOR

Corporations often wish to educate their employees as a way of motivating and retaining good talent. Classes on financial management, tax planning, estate planning, and even physical fitness, nutrition, and quitting smoking are popular. If you own a day spa, educate on stress reduction. If you own a martial arts training facility or security company, educate on personal and company safety. Also, government regulations (the Employee Retirement Income Security Act of 1974 (ERISA), Sec. 404c) require employers to "educate" their employees regarding the choices they must make within their fringe benefit package. The requirement to "educate" employees remains undefined in the statute. Is it simply furnishing a fact sheet on the available investment choices? Or is the requirement to "educate" better fulfilled by a helpful and comprehensive class on personal financial planning that provides a road map to making their uniquely correct selections? As an employer, I want the latter, especially as the definition of "educate" is left to case law, meaning the courts.

Any knowledge to be imparted about health care, insurance, or retirement plan choices is desired by employers to meet their statutory fiduciary requirements. But many employers are seeking classes to truly help their employees beyond that suggested by law. If you can help people live their lives more fully, with greater safety or enhanced enjoyment, do not neglect the opportunity to educate in the workplace.

Gain an Organizational Sponsor

An organizational sponsor is especially valuable if you provide your service business-to-business rather than to consumers. As an actuary or retirement plan administrator, every industry group may sponsor your educational seminar in your area from contractors to dentists to undertakers. And those disciplines that provide services to consumers can also find fertile fields in industry and business organizations. However, remember that you are still speaking to people, so your talk must be directed to what benefits them. Do not talk about the trends in underwriting for long-term care insurance when you should be speaking on what a nursing home stay does to a family's finances.

Use Quality Instructional Material

Instructional material does not have to be expensively prepared, but it does have to be professional and reflect well on you. This means you must take the time to prepare yourself properly and create compelling instructional materials. If you cannot do this, buy good course outlines and materials. It is a solid investment because your reason for teaching is to demonstrate your competence and trustworthiness. Be sure to convey that by providing the right experience for the attendees and sponsors.

TEACHING THE SEMINARS

Many psychological studies have been done on stress and the undesirable activities and events that cause stress. Most of those studies rank public speaking as a stress inducer close to losing a job or even a loved one. That sounds extreme, but public speaking does not appeal to many people. Examining why this occurs may be helpful in overcoming this unreasoned fear. Most of us had to get up in front of the class in elementary school to recite or do math problems. The tender sensibilities of the young speaker were assailed by the smirks and whispered comments of classmates. This was all in good fun and turn around was fair play, but wounding nonetheless. As a 16-year-old, I had to address the *entire school* in an assembly. My knees were literally knocking. One of those teachers I acknowledged at the beginning of this book, Bill Kohler, gave sage advice to control my breathing, and that helped some. But it was very fortunate that I had a lectern in front of me to hide my knocking knees and to allow me to hold on to stay upright. I'm sure that my voice covered an entire octave as I spoke and that was not because of controlled modulation. If that is also your background experience, you are blanching at my suggestion to give educational lectures to gain new clients or customers. Believe me, it does not work that way as an adult. As Franklin Roosevelt said, you have nothing to fear but fear itself.

Here's why. First, you know everything about your business and your subject matter. Your audience may know some, but not nearly as much as you. Yes, you may have students who think they do, but you can politely overcome and quickly deflect that intrusion based on your more substantive knowledge of the subject. Second, you will have prepared your presentation material properly because this is not extemporaneous speaking, and you will have practiced. Third, your audience, unlike my high school friends, will personally and immediately benefit from what you are presenting. Finally, if you are truly committed to public speaking as a way of demonstrating your business knowledge, you can invest in yourself by enrolling in a course like the Dale Carnegie course in public speaking. I took the course years ago, and one of my classmates was so fearful of public speaking that he would get up in front of our friendly class only if he could put his hands over his face while speaking! By the end of the several week program, he was delivering talks with face uncovered and receiving the accolades of his fellow class members. You are likely not that fearful, but even one who is can become an accomplished speaker with training and practice. The payoff is worth the effort, both in terms of business gained and in personal achievement.

Here are the components of effective public speaking.

1. *Prepare your material.* Your speaking notes should be premade and you must practice. Give your talk in an empty room and, once you are comfortable with your presentation, give it before a friendly audience of two or three people. Their job is not to be critical, but to simply be an audience. If you want to improve, enlist an experienced coach or enroll in a program for improving.

2. *Prepare the speaking room and venue.* Make sure that you are familiar with the room in which you will be speaking. Where possible, have an assistant to greet and register attendees so that you are free to mentally prepare. Let your assistant deal with the questions about registration, parking, directions for class, and the like. This also helps to instill your imagery with attendees as their instructor. Make sure that your equipment works properly before the first student arrives. A burned-out projector bulb will detract from the experience for you and for the students. Make sure that you have a spare for anything that could burn out or wear out. Have an extra extension cord in case the room is not what you expected.

3. *Prepare yourself mentally.* You are the instructor, and these are adults. You are no longer in elementary school so, although the attendees are interested in who you are, they are not rooting for you to fail. They are there to gain beneficial knowledge, and you are the one from whom they are seeking it.

   And here is a big key to success. Get outside of yourself. This is not at all about you. It is about the attendees. Focus on them and your material without any concept of self entering into your thought process. If you mentally ask yourself if you are coming across well, you have strayed over the line to ruinous self-inspection. Think only of your class and if they are learning. Watch faces and respond to what you see in them. As I tell the instructors at our firm, you should be able to look down halfway through class and realize only then that you forgot to put on your trousers or your skirt—you should be that much into your students and your message. Do not second-guess yourself, because you are prepared and knowledgeable.

4. *Be physically prepared.* Dress properly and well. Better to be over-formally dressed than under. People do judge you by your appearance, and good grooming, clean clothing, and appropriate dress will keep you from worrying over your appearance. Scuffed shoes, a plunging dress neckline, or being badly in need of a haircut will detract from your students' opinion of you as a competent professional.

    A story relayed by one of our retired clients illustrates the danger of dressing for personal convenience versus for professionalism. This retired husband and wife changed dentists because their long-time professional had taken to wearing chinos and golf shirts to the office instead of his traditional lab coat. Sound silly or maybe just an isolated example? It is not silly if you lose patients, clients, or customers because you appeared to disrespect them with unprofessional dress. And it is not isolated, I can assure you. That was only one story of many that could have been included here. Professional dress is not always synonymous with a lab coat or business suit. The key is to dress appropriately for your clients and your professional stature, not for your own convenience. But with lectures, business dress is required.

5. *Be yourself.* An inexperienced public speaker often unconsciously imitates the demeanor and style of his or her college professors. Although it is an educational seminar, your professors or, worse, their graduate assistants are not role models for what you are trying to do here. In college, the instructor is delivering material—take it or leave it. With educational seminars for adults who may become your clients, you are trying

to help them learn. So if you are to imitate any of your past instructors, copy the most caring and most effective high-school teacher you experienced. Your caring that your students learn will include the inference that you will care if they are successful when participating in the services you provide.

6. *Educate, don't sell.* Remember that this is not about you. It is about the attendees and what they want from life. By giving the best educational experience possible, you do the best job of selling yourself. You do not have to talk about you to convey the impression that you are competent. Just the opposite. Educate properly, and they will know you are competent. But also remember that you are not educating do-it-yourselfers, so you are not obligated to provide a verbal or written instruction manual. The objective is to identify individual goals and create a plan to achieve them—regardless of your field. Educated clients are the best clients because they subscribe to your principles and strategies. But they are still supposed to become clients and not competitors. You are greatly aided in this with properly prepared material that will help keep you on track.

For the personal service provider who is new in business as well as the experienced pro, educational seminars remain the best way to gain qualified new clients.

REFERRALS

Gaining referrals is the best way to market. A referral comes to you predisposed to become your client or customer based on the good experience and recommendation of someone that person trusts. That referrer may be one of your clients, another professional, one of your seminar sponsors, or someone you impressed with your sincerely accomplished networking. The paradox of referrals is that they are the best way to market, but you will not get referrals until you have used the other methods of marketing yourself. So how do you gain referrals?

The primary way is by being referable. That means doing the following things:

- Doing the best quality work possible for your clients and customers
- Being honest in all of your dealings
- Preserving client confidentiality
- Providing referrals to others

No one will refer to a provider of poor quality workmanship or service or someone who cannot hold a confidence or who is seemingly less than fully honest and straightforward. It would be unusual for someone to refer a service provider who is disorganized, slovenly, or ill mannered and thus would prove to be an embarrassment. Work at being referable because a referral is a reflection on the person making the referral. Act, look, and speak well, and your clients will want to show you off to their friends, family, and associates.

But most of all, to gain referrals you should be a prolific referrer yourself to other compatible disciplines and even to your clients. An attorney refers to an accountant who refers to a financial advisor who refers to the others in return. We have all heard and understood the phrase "priming the pump." That refers to the act of pouring some water down a pump to make water come back out in a flow. That is how referrals work. But you will not get back referrals in exactly the same proportion as you gave them or in a preset time period. Not to worry. As long as you are referring to quality people and they are doing a good job for your clients and friends whom you referred, the returns will inevitably come. Meanwhile, you did not refer out simply to get back. You referred to other professionals because you felt your referrals would be properly serviced and that is reason enough. Your clients were properly handled, and the rest will happen naturally in its own time.

You can also refer out to your clients in addition to other professionals in the community. If your client owns a restaurant serving good food, refer people to it. If your client is a chiropractor who provides quality care, refer potential patients to him. You are helping the people you refer and your clients. Life is, after all, a mirror. The reflection we cast is the one that comes back to us. Gaining referrals from clients is heavily dependent on good quality service, and it has been said that clients fall into the following three categories:

1. Those who will always refer without being asked. We bless them, as they are intrinsically good people who want to help you and their friends who they are referring to your good service.

2. Those who do not naturally refer but would if properly asked and if a comfortable way of accomplishing this were provided. This is your greatest opportunity, and we will return to this group momentarily.

3. Those who will never refer, no matter how good your service. They are private people who may appreciate your service but are not comfortable talking to others no matter how you encourage or reward it. Fortunately, this is the smallest group. And sometimes, they do change their minds and occasionally morph to the middle group.

All three groups have to be serviced properly because that is the contract you entered into when you accepted them as clients or customers. And the methods you employ to motivate them to refer and to reward that action are uniformly applied.

The following paragraphs describe some of the methods we have used to gain referrals.

We meet with our clients at least annually and many times as often as quarterly. Once we have gone through the review process, and the clients have had all of their questions answered and are comfortable with our handling of their accounts, we ask for referrals. We mention that our business comes to us from our educational seminars and from referrals, and that we do not waste time that we can be spending on their behalf with cold calling or other such actions. So we appreciate their confidence in us and would be flattered by their expression of that confidence in referring family, friends, and business associates. We promise to treat their referrals with the same respect as we do them and to preserve the confidentiality of both parties. We do not press this, but simply state it, and it is well received. An honest expression of your feelings and a straightforward request makes the process comfortable for the client and the service provider.

The educational lectures are an ideal forum for gaining referrals. It is quite easy to encourage clients to bring family and friends to the educational institution-sponsored lectures. We publicize the schedule in our client newsletters and offer a workbook discount coupon for clients and their invited guests. The presence of the client and guest at our lecture is the referral. It is up to us to then demonstrate our competence to that guest as well as to all of the other attendees of that class to convert them to clients.

We use special seminars and events. Here is where the dinner seminar at the club or hotel works well. This is presented as a client appreciation event where they have the opportunity of bringing family and friends. The implicit referral and outcome are the same as with the educational seminar, but it has a much more exclusive-to-clients feel about it, not better just different. The topic can induce the result. For example, we have given a special lecture entitled, "What Parents and their Grown Children Should Discuss." This clearly points to both the invited guests and to the expected outcome. It is an ideal way for a 35-year-old client to cause her 65-year-old parents to begin a dialogue over estate and long-term care planning. In reverse, the retired client can stop nagging his 35- year-old dentist son to begin his children's education funding and a retirement plan because our class provides that instruction and motivation for him. We have done a brief lecture prior to a ball game where we had a private box. (It's not as expensive as you might think, especially if your hometown team isn't having a winning season.) The theme of the lecture was built around baseball. We likened to the fielding of a complete team in a ball game to coordinating one's advisory team and investment management approach. People had fun, and it spurred discussion. Clients brought family and close friends to hear the talk and then enjoy the game. The success of this type of effort will be proportional to the preparation and follow-up that you put into it.

Referral contests work well. I must admit to trepidation over this idea when it was first presented to us by our advertising and public relations agency, Krakoff Communications. Jeff Krakoff convinced us to try it as it had worked well for some of his other clients. It somehow seemed wrong for us just as the dinner certificate raffle had seemed wrong when initially suggested years ago in spurring data form submission from our lectures. In both cases, I was fearful that it would be construed as somehow nonprofessional or even tacky. That was not the case with either initiative. Our clients got into the spirit of the contest and had lots of fun with it. Here's how it worked.

We publicized the contest for a specified period of three months. In that outreach, we explained that our business grows from referrals from satisfied clients because we do not cold call. We appreciate our clients' confidence in us, and we urge them to make our quality of service available to their family, friends, business associates, and neighbors. Including that list of possible referrals is important because it opens up the client's thinking to the full range of possibilities. We mentioned that we would send them a modest gift of appreciation for each referral they submitted. For this, we used our logo items beginning with a coffee mug and progressing up through caps, athletic t-shirts, and sweatshirts through golf shirts and clocks with each additional referral. If a referred person became a client, that would provide the referrer with a ticket in the grand prizes raffle, as would each subsequent referral that became a client.

We asked them to tell the referred person about the referral and that we would call them. That is a key ingredient for the success of the program, both for us in gaining clients and for the referrer who would be given a grand prize ticket for the new client. Several grand prizes were to be given, and every ticket qualified for each prize. We were careful to not exceed Internal Revenue Service (IRS) and industry regulatory limits in the value of the prizes, but there were enough prizes that every multiple referrer received something. The referrer with the largest number of referrals was photographed receiving the prize and placed in our quarterly newsletter.

Let me remind you that I was very reluctant to do this program because I felt the way you may be feeling now as you read this. But my concerns were quickly dispelled when I saw how enthusiastically our clients participated in this program. Your clients really do want to help you, and a program like this allows them an avenue and a focus for doing so. And they have fun along the way. It was a great success, gaining many referrals and many new clients. Thank you, Jeff Krakoff, for helping me see the light. This will become an annual event, but we will try to invent new twists each year so it does not become stale. Maybe we'll tie the awards to a client appreciation event. That way, every client attending will see the benefit of referring in real time.

We use sporting events to reward prolifically referring professionals and clients. Each of our financial consultants stake claim to one of the season's games to use our four season tickets for Pittsburgh Steelers football. They invite referring accountants, attorneys, and other professionals. Clients who refer also qualify for this perk. The time spent in brunch before and at the game solidifies the relationship and lets the referring party know how highly we value their confidence in us. And it is a fun way to spend a weekend afternoon with people we like.

It bears repeating that referrals will come *after* you have gained clients. The other methods for acquiring clients must be used first, and referral techniques as outlined can be practiced as a natural outflow of those other efforts. Do not neglect referral initiatives, because they are golden paths for growing your business.

CHAPTER THIRTEEN

MANAGING YOUR BUSINESS

This will be an important body of information once you have started your business and gained a meaningful client or customer base. Yet, it is also important to keep these principles in mind as you build the business and acquire clients. It is far less disruptive to begin with an efficiently structured client management system that is conducive to profitability than to have to create systems, drastically restructure, and then jettison clients later.

THE PUGIL STICK EFFECT

We named this tactic after an interesting bit of military training. Years ago, the author underwent one of the most productive character building exercises ever devised. It was and still is called Recruit Training at Parris Island, South Carolina, through the U.S. Marine Corps. The author was fortunate to have had friends undergo this training prior to his time there, so forewarned was, literally, forearmed. A good friend then and now is Bill Schroeder. Today, Bill is our lending officer for our account at his bank. Then he was a good childhood friend.

To digress for a moment, I believe this story also illustrates another business management maxim. Where possible, make sure that your relationships endure. That is not always possible but, when it is, the history, trust, and friendship will make life more fun and mutually profitable. That certainly is true now when Bill Schroeder as our banker does not need to relearn who we are, and we can trust his word as his bond.

One of many helpful advance advisories that Bill delivered about Marine recruit training concerned the pugil stick course. This is where recruits wear a football helmet, a groin pad, and hold a heavy, long stick that is covered on both ends with padding. It looks like a huge Q-tip. But if hit with it, one can be knocked off one's feet or at least have one's innards rattled. It is meant to simulate rifle with fixed bayonet combat and can be quite sobering when considered that way. The instructors spent considerable time teaching the finer techniques of thrust, parry, slice, and stroke—horizontal butt strike, vertical butt stroke, slash, and ongoing like an accomplished fencer. But Bill levied sound advice to ignore all of that and just go whale away at the adversary. Don't make it pretty, Bill advised, just knock him off his feet as soon as possible with an unrelenting, blurring battering of swings. Bill was right. I became the platoon champ, and it took three people engaged at the same time to knock me off my feet. Two couldn't do it. I was certainly not that tough. But the concept of going full tilt toward a goal with unremitting tenacity allowed me to overcome stronger opponents who were distracted with making sure they used proper technique and who were cautiously prethinking every move. It was a valuable lesson that has stayed with me. It can also to apply to business.

Many times we encounter the calculating person who wishes to evaluate in advance all of the details of an initiative or encounter. That is not possible as events unfold too rapidly and in unexpected ways. And the individual often talks him- or herself out of trying at all. Life is what happens while you are making plans, and you cannot envision every twist and turn in the road toward your goal. Yes, you do need to evaluate expected reward and risk in any endeavor. But if you think that business, like a pugil stick fight, will follow the guidebook and feel that you need to choreograph every step in advance, you are limiting your potential rewards. You may find yourself never getting started or talking yourself out of some really great opportunities simply because you cannot envision the steps and outcome in detail. So, if the reward is worth the effort, and the risk seems assumable, go out and whale away at the opportunity, and don't worry about catching a hit or two. It probably will not be fatal.

That accept-no-defeat mentality will serve you well as you sally forward to build your business and your client base. But managing your business will require a bit more circumspection, which is the topic for this chapter. This is not contradictory because you must work for success and then consolidate it once it has been achieved. This way, you will not lose that which was gained, and it will help you to build further on it.

MANAGE YOUR BUSINESS OR IT WILL MANAGE YOU

In the *E-Myth Revisited,* Michael Gerber presents a clear distinction between highly skilled technicians (be they patent attorneys, accountants, or watchmakers) who begin a business only to find that they are consumed by the hours and simply have traded one form of master for another. The clients or customers who control their lives have replaced their former employers' control of them. You will not own your business, it will own you, but only if you let it. Controlling your business through good management involves three areas:

1. Activities and time management
2. People management
3. Client or customer management

We will cover each of these and then end this chapter with lessons learned concerning managing in tough times.

TIME MANAGEMENT

Time management is really activities management. Please read that sentence again. We cannot "manage" time as we all have the same amount of time available to us each day. Rather, we must manage what we do with that time. The quality of results from your daily efforts will be directly proportionate to the activities that you engage in during the day. There are many good time management books, and this section is an attempt to distill the author's reading and experience for you.

Let us begin by debunking the scheduling school of time management. It is not practical to exactly schedule your telephone calling time or your playtime with your children. You will see shortly that those *activities* should be accommodated in your planning, but not the exact time of the day or week when they will occur. To attempt to do so is to court failure and help ensure disappointment with your results. Now we will move to a short course in activities' management. Be aware that these are a distillation of many ideas, but that they are part of a cohesive *system*. And that is the key. *Managing your activities and use of time for your business and personal success is not an eclectic grouping of time management ideas. Instead, it is a mindset resulting in a systemic approach to the attainment of what you want in life.*

ACTIVITIES MANAGEMENT

Why do this? Because activities management is the best way to reach your objectives. Harvard University studied a group of its graduates 20 years after receiving their degrees. It found that the 3 percent of the grads who had written goals and plans of action out-earned the other 97 percent! That forms a powerful statement for an organized, written approach to activities management. The alternative to activities' management is to take it as it comes. Although the ability to adapt and improvise is a valuable trait, it implies the assumption that one is adapting and improvising from a plan, not within chaos.

Another reason we must learn and practice effective activities management is that we are multifaceted beings. We have goals and responsibilities tied to the following:

- Self
- Family

- Spirituality
- Career

We must, therefore, learn to compartmentalize and balance sometimes seemingly competing goals and demands. The only solution is to manage. The alternatives to managing are (a) chaos, and/or (b) downsizing our lives and accepting less than we are capable of achieving. In your sunset years, you likely will feel better about having accomplished all that you desired in all of the preceding four areas instead of having settled for only a small portion.

So, how do we do this? We accomplish activities management in three steps:

1. Determine your **goals.**

2. **Prioritize** your activities to coincide *only* with your goals.

3. **Organize** your time to accommodate your highest and best goals' activities.

That is all there is. Avoid activities and influences that distract you and detract from your goals' accomplishment. Think about the alternative using the analogy of food consumption. How would you feel about a person who ate everything that came within his or her view? Whatever food catches the eye becomes part of the meal. How would you feel about that glutton's character? How would that person's body look? How healthy would he or she be? It is the same with the use of time. Many activities look attractive. But to do whatever comes into one's field of vision is, at best, childish. At worst, it is self-defeating.

SELF

You must take care of your own needs, or you will be less effective for all other areas of your life. Learning new skills, taking vacations, and diversionary activities all play a part in this. Creating these as goals and then scheduling activities to accomplish them forms both a means for self-actualization as well as for meaningful relaxation. This is necessary for a complete life and as a balance to a challenging work environment.

In addition, it is essential that your personal habits contribute to an increased energy level and a positive outlook on life. That means avoiding recreational drugs and the over-use of alcohol. Do not use tobacco in any form. It means regular exercise and adequate sleep. It also includes the infusion of positive reading, movies, and television. You cannot retreat from the realities of the world. But if you fill your recreational time with unhealthy activities and your thoughts with consistently negative imagery, it will inevitably detract from your energy, your enthusiasm, and your ability to deal effectively with the really important goals that you wish to attain. Joel Weldon, a popular motivational speaker, coined the phrase, "Junk food/junk body and junk thoughts/junk mind." Eat poorly and you will have a poorly functioning body. Fill your mind with rot, and you will have a very hard time in positively actualizing your life's goals.

The good news is that you do not have to exist exclusively on roots and berries to eat well. There are three simple rules for good eating:

1. *Eat a well-balanced diet.* That means all of the recommended food groups should be adequately represented in each day's diet.

2. *Eat as close to natural as possible.* Processed foods are far worse for your health and waistline than naturally occurring foods like butter, eggs, and unprocessed cheese. Seek whole grain bread and pasta products as opposed to those made with processed white flour. Potential harm in a food is directly proportional to the amount of factory processing it received. Also, how an animal that is providing you with nourishment was raised and fed impacts its benefit or harm to you. A calf penned in a small crate for its entire young life and given a watery mixture of milk and antibiotics is not going to provide you with healthful nourishment, even if the veal industry tells you it will. Seek naturally raised animals, poultry, or fish in an

attempt to factor out all of the additives that do your body no good.

3. *Eat reasonably sized portions.* Eat more frequently in controlled portions if you become hungry. Do not skip meals or overeat at a sitting.

Read the diet books if you wish. But, based on my experience and study, the three preceding rules, coupled with adequate exercise, will serve you as well.

EXERCISE

Exercise is a vital component of healthy living. The good news about exercise, like eating, is that it should not involve a radical approach. Dr. Kenneth Cooper is an internationally known physician who started Americans jogging and running in the early 1970s with his book *Aerobics.* Its findings resulted from Dr. Cooper's research as an U.S. Air Force physician studying human performance related to flight. Cooper tells us that, if we are running more than three miles, three times per week, we are running for reasons beyond fitness. He and most other experts in the field counsel alternating running or other aerobic activities such as biking and cross-country skiing with weight-lifting exercise. And as most experts counsel, brisk daily walking can form the mainstay of a solid exercise regimen. The weight component can be added and exercise intensity raised by doing light, hand-held dumbbell exercises while walking.

FAMILY

We often hear the comment that family is more important than work. That should certainly be true of us all. However, that comment is usually delivered in the context that career must suffer in favor of family. Yet, on closer examination, we may find that same person watching every situation comedy and sporting event that is televised. Is this really a competition between family and work or something else? It is possible to raise accomplished and loving children and have a successful career. When my children were growing up, one of the written goals I kept in my personal planner was to help raise accomplished and complete human beings. I am very proud to say that all three of my daughters met and exceed that definition. I never missed one important event in their upbringing, regardless of schedule and participated meaningfully in their growing and shaping. Yet, I watched very little television with them. The point is to have a mindset of meeting our responsibility to participate meaningfully with our children and to parent them, not a dictating of what should and should not be done together. Like every other aspect of your life, your goals regarding family should reflect the desired end result, and your activities should then be pointed toward the attainment of those goals. This will be true for you and your spouse or life partner also.

Here is an example. I spoke with my daughter, Kathy, on a recent Saturday, and she and her husband, Mike, and children, Katie and Bailey, were headed outside to shovel snow together. As soon as they finished their driveway, they were going to shovel the drive of an elderly neighbor who was recovering from knee surgery. That is matching activities with goals for children's proper upbringing. It does not have to be a spectacular, once-in-a-lifetime activity. You only need to choose your daily activities to coincide with what you want for your family.

SPIRITUALITY

This is often correctly thought to be synonymous with the practice of religion. That is certainly an apt connection. But in terms of your fulfillment, it is suggested that you broaden that definition to include gaining an understanding of people and how they live and work together as well to frame a concept of how you believe the world works. For many people, their religion is intrinsic to those two points. However, with or without a strong religious conviction, a well-grounded feeling about people and the world will make you both more interesting and more effective in your progression toward your goals.

CAREER

That is what this book is all about. You will have a running start in this section based on the work that you did earlier in the book with the two questions of "What do I want to do every day?" and "With whom do I want to do it?" Your goals for your career will be clear and succinct. But again, be sure to include those traveling life's path with you in the formulation of these goals.

ALL AREAS OF YOUR LIFE

You can have it all if you wish it. The gaining will not be without bumps in the road as those are a given whether you try or not. But a clearly articulated statement and a system for accomplishing your personal, family, spiritual, and career goals is the best and most assured way to make them happen.

PUTTING YOUR GOALS INTO ACTION

Now, how do we go about this? First, determine and write down goals for each important area of your life. These goals must be *specific and measurable.* A goal cannot be vague, such as, "make a lot of money." You cannot plan for such vagueness, and your progress or even attainment cannot be measured. And do not set goals too low. You are not trying to get through each day; you are trying to accomplish something. We are often admonished to not set goals too high. And there can be some validity to that if "too high" means arbitrary and unrealistic. If your sales are $100,000 this year, and you arbitrarily set a goal for $1 million in sales for next year that may be simply wishful thinking. The problem with that particular goal is not likely the $1 million figure. It is the time frame and, more importantly, the lack of thought and planning prior to setting it. So the error is not in setting goals too high, it is not planning properly for their achievement.

Consider some example of goals in the four life goals categories.

These are only examples and meant to be illustrative in your thoughtful planning.

PERSONAL

- Gain specialized knowledge, like learning another language
- Learn a new discipline, as with a sport or craft
- Lose weight and inches
- Heighten state of physical fitness, measured by distance, speed, weights lifted, and the frequency of such activity
- Travel to specified destinations or at specified times of the upcoming year
- Reduce stress by engaging in specific activities such as yoga, reading, meditation, or contemplation

FAMILY

- Raise responsible and well-rounded children by interacting and sharing activities in the following manner: _____ _____ and with the following frequency: _____.
- Begin and continue prefunding your children's higher education. Specify amounts and frequency and for what period of time.
- Plan for interactive time with spouse or partner in the following manner: _____.
- Do specific home remodeling projects that enhance family life.

SPIRITUALITY

- Practice your religion in the following manner: _____ _____ and with the following frequency: _____.

- Gain better insight into human nature through reading or investigating in the following manner: _____ .

- Associate with or remove from association those identified people who can help or hurt your efforts at self-betterment.

- Enroll in an educational course.

CAREER

- Outline goals for your business in terms of the upcoming year's revenues and profits.

- Acquire specific assets or resources for the business.

- Plan a personal level of income for the upcoming year or a stepped goal for the next several years. Longer-term goals, for example dealing with your income in 10 years, are not helpful unless they also contain subgoals for each intervening year.

- Gain a specific skill or additional specific knowledge

These are illustrative and will not necessary be the goals that you will select. But notice that each is specific as to time frame and action required. Vague statements, although potentially motivational, will not be helpful. You can now begin to fashion your own specific and measurable goals in each of those areas. The absence of clear and written goals will greatly diminish your chances of ever attaining what you truly want. Hark back to Napoleon Hill's time-tested admonition that we can achieve whatever we can conceive and believe. This is the time when you must start conceiving, and then you can begin believing. Once you know what you want, you can set about achieving it.

The first of our three-step goal achievement exercise was to identify our goals. The second step is to now prioritize our activities to coincide with the attainment of those goals. Remembering the glutton, we know that we cannot become involved with every activity that comes before us. Only those activities that assist us in getting what we want should be fitted into our valuable 24-hour day and 7-day week. Sound joyless? Lack spontaneity? Not at all! What is joyless is failing

to get what you want and deserve from life and looking back with disappointment. Lack of spontaneity is letting others dictate your activities and your life and feeling controlled. Now, that is really
depressing. What you are doing in ordering your activities in line
with your true goals is taking control of your life rather than abrogat-
ing that control to others.

Now write every one of your goals as a column heading and then
list the activities that you must perform to reach those goals. You
sheet should look like the following.

Area of Life	Goal	Activity	Time Frame
Personal	Better health and fitness	Run a 10K race	Begin training and adhere to the following early morning, daily training schedule
Family	Closeness with children	Weekly family night with differing venues	Every Sunday evening. Family votes on activity each Saturday
Spirituality	Grow in faith	Church services. Men's discussion group	Weekly on Saturday Bi-monthly
Career	Start own personal service business	Planning Implementation	Two evenings weekly for three months. A definitive schedule of activities necessary and time frame.

Reflect on the preceding examples. There are not several goals
for each area of life. This allows for maximum focus on your most important goals. Once achieved, you can add other goals as they become appropriate. Do not overload your schedule with too many
competing activities or fragment your focus from the most important
and immediate of your goals.

Also, be prepared for others to criticize your goals, your methods,
and your adherence to your plan. You can counter this in two ways.

First, do not share your thoughts and planning with those who are not integral to its success. Your spouse, life partner, children, parents, and business partner should be made aware and enlisted as allies in the accomplishment of your goals as they are impacted by them. Others who cannot assist should not become part of the process. They will see the results soon enough and bringing them into your thoughts and conversation prematurely will only serve as a distraction. You do not need corroboration of your goals, as they are uniquely yours.

The second way to counter interference with your goals is to not associate with those who would drag you down emotionally or criticize your initiative. Think about the type of comments you may hear like, "Hey! You're going to get too good for us!" Or, "We came from the same neighborhood. None of our people have ever done that." Or, the common indictment, "You're going to neglect your family with all of that business activity." That is mind clutter coming from folks who are unwilling to try and who want to justify their lack of effort. When I have been admonished to "stop and smell the roses" my response has always been, "Whose roses, yours or mine?" Usually when someone says that, they have a clear impression of how they wish you to live your life. But the definition of "roses" is very individual, and only you can decide what is important to you. You know what you want and that you will meet all of your obligations along the way. You have planned and prioritized. Go for it, and then you can adapt and improvise from your plan as you go when the inevitable unforeseen instances occur. None of that will get you off track because you know where you want to go.

The third and last step is to plan your daily and weekly activities so that you are adhering to your goal-oriented plan. This daily and weekly system can be managed in any way that best suits your style. The tools you use will conform to your preferences and technical skills level. That means you can use a paper or an electronic planner. You can be networked with coworkers in your business or use an individual system. Regardless of the system you use, the following characteristics are not optional. A viable system should include the following.

First, *make time to plan your day and your week.* People who have studied this claim, and my experience makes me agree that each hour planned garners a multiple of that time in increased efficiency. After you have finished this section, try what I am recommending, and I believe you will agree also. If you wish to succeed, you do not have time *not* to plan because you have none to waste with non-goal-oriented activities.

Second, *delegate or ignore all non-goal-oriented activities.* Quite a few years ago, a computer specialist I had hired as an independent contractor was working on an important project for me. His stated goal was to break free of his corporate employer and own and operate his own computer consulting business. Meanwhile, he was working evenings and weekends to build a clientele and his consulting reputation. That was clearly his stated goal. In the middle of the project, he told me that he could not work on an upcoming Saturday—because he had to clean his garage. It had gotten very cluttered, and his wife was nagging him to organize and clean it. At that time, I was paying him $40 per hour, and he could have paid his teenage son $10 per hour to sort the garage. And maybe his son would have done a better job of it. That example speaks for itself, and, the results do too. He is not in business for himself even after all these years. And the people I hired thereafter, Moir Computer Services, have been doing our computer work admirably and capably for the last 16 years and have earned tens of thousands of dollars in consulting fees during that period of time. The original consultant should have learned to delegate properly and to focus on his goals.

Third, *understand and use points of control.* In any endeavor, we must ask and answer the question, "Who has the point of control?" That means who has the responsibility of guiding this along? In any project that you initiate, you first have the point of control. Once you delegate to others, they have the point of control—but only if they have the same cause of motivation as you. Two examples will clarify this concept.

If I delegate a project or action to a coworker, he or she has the point of control and the corresponding authority and responsibility for completing the task. That assumes that I delegated it to the proper person in my organization who is qualified and properly equipped to make it happen. If so, *I must relinquish the point of control to him or her.* To not do so undermines that individual and also keeps me tied to the project. If I wanted that, I wouldn't have decided to delegate it. We must all learn to award the point of control and step back, provided that the person we award it to has the same motivation and is able to accomplish the mission.

By contrast, I can never relinquish the point of control to anyone who does not share my cause of motivation, regardless how well qualified. Consider the example of a prospect who promises to accomplish the next step in becoming a client, maybe by completing a new client data form or account paperwork. If I award the point of control to that prospect, it may be weeks before I remember that the assignment was not completed. It is my job, or my designee's job within my organization, to follow up on that necessary action. I cannot abrogate that responsibility by giving the prospect my point of control. If this sounds simple or overdone, I would ask that you think back on recent delays in turning a prospect into a client or customer. I'll bet inappropriately giving that prospect the point of control had something to do with it.

Fourth, *write everything down.* Do not trust your memory. Your mental hard drive is not big enough to hold everything that it must to successfully run a business. Also, writing things forms a record for later checking on completion or for clarifying misunderstood communications. We use a catch phrase in our company to remind associates who forget this rule. When we are discussing something that will need action and remembering and the associate is not taking notes, we simply ask, "You'll remember this, huh?" That usually results in an immediate and large grin and the appearance of a pen and notebook or daily planner.

Last, *prioritize those activities that you legitimately hold for yourself to do.* The story is told that, in the early 1900s, Charles Schwab, the legendary steel company executive paid a consultant the then princely sum of $10,000 for a management idea that supposedly revolutionized his activities management. Here it is.

IT IS AS EASY AS A-B-C

All of your activities may be reduced to a categorization designated by A, B, or C. Some systems use A, B, C, and D. No matter, use what works for you. But here is the system that I have used for years. When I use it consistently, I am very effective. When time pressures cause me to omit this, and we are all human, I become less effective. The key is to employ this methodology as consistently as possible. Every activity must carry an A, B, or C designation. You can use a paper planner or an electronic one. I use both. The paper planner is for my personal use, and it is always with me. It also contains my list of personal, family, spiritual, and career and business goals. It contains important other data like family Social Security numbers and airline frequent flyer account numbers. It has a synopsis of our annual budget and much more. In addition, our firm uses an electronic scheduling system wherein we are all networked, and our receptionist can efficiently schedule us. That shared electronic system also allows me to efficiently delegate the scheduling of appointments to her and frees me from the inevitable telephone tag and multiple date discussion calls that would detract from my primary goal-oriented activities. So use what works for you, which may be one or two systems depending on your interaction within your company.

The definition that I give to the A-B-C designations is unique to my business. However, yours should not look different in order of importance. Only the wording will vary from mine.

A   Only those activities that immediately and directly relate to my objectives. For example, closing a new client for the firm or beneficially impacting our portfolio management results.

B   Those activities that put me on a clear path to achieving my results. An example would be preparing for a client closing meeting or researching and discussing an investment we will use.

C   Everything else. This runs the gamut of getting a haircut to listening to an associate's story of a weekend trip. If it is not an A or a B, then it is a C because it will not help you realize your goals.

Consider the trick we often play on ourselves. We say that we will clear all of those Cs so we will have time for the really important things. What we have in fact done is to fill our days with unimportant and non-goal-oriented activities. Having your automobile inspected, getting a haircut, and cleaning your garage must be placed on your schedule in an appropriate order of importance. And better yet, properly delegated (except for the haircut).

TECHNIQUES OF ACTIVITIES MANAGEMENT

The daily planning system that you use will be, as mentioned, up to you. But the way in which you use it may resemble the system in Figure 13.1. Your activities will fall into the following three areas:

1. Meetings/appointments
2. Calls
3. Actions

And each activity will carry an A, B, or C designation. We will use a typical daily planner book format to illustrate how this can be implemented.

Your planner might also contain space for recording notes for each activity performed and the time spent,which is also an effective tool in evaluating your time usage. But we will eliminate that for simplicity's sake in Figure 13.2. Filled in, your daily planner sheet may look like Figure 13.3.

These are typical entries. Note that only the appointment column carries time slots. The calls and actions are timeless and to be performed during the day as we see them at this point. But to make this meaningful and prioritized, the entries should look like this.

One may view this sheet and conclude that it represents too much work or unnecessary work. Consider what is likely to happen if this sheet is not completed this way. Typically, the friend's lunch appointment would be made, the home repairs scheduled, and the

Time	Appointments	Telephone Calls	Actions	Comments
7:00 a.m.				
7:30				
8:00				
8:30				
9:00				
9:30				
10:00				
10:30				
11:00				
11:30				
12:00 p.m.				
12:30				
1:00				
1:30				
2:00				
2:30				
3:00				
3:30				
4:00				
4:30				
5:00				

Figure 13.1   Basic Daily Planning System

Time	Appointments	Telephone Calls	Actions
7:00 a.m.		Appleby	Buy Shoes
7:30		Friday	Finish planning for Thatcher meeting
8:00		McDonald	
8:30		Alby	
9:00		Burger	
9:30	Smith, Richard		
10:00			
10:30			
11:00			
11:30			
12:00 p.m.			
12:30			
1:00			
1:30	Jones, Robert		
2:00			
2:30			
3:00	Brown, Donald		
3:30			
4:00			
4:30			
5:00			

Figure 13.2   Daily Planner with Notes

Time	Priority	Appointments	Priority	Telephone Calls	Priority	Actions
7:00 a.m.			A	Appleby (discuss investment recommendations)	C	Buy shoes
7:30					B	Finish planning for Thatcher meeting (recommendations for investing)
8:00			A	Friday (follow up on investment recommendations)		
8:30						
9:00			B	McDonald (possible seminar sponsor)		
9:30	A	Smith, Richard (deliver financial plan)				
10:00			C	Alby (friend-lunch appointment)		
10:30			C	Burger (arrange home repairs)		
11:00						
11:30						
12:00 p.m.						
12:30						
1:00						
1:30	A	Jones, Robert (deliver financial plan)				
2:00						
2:30						
3:00	B	Brown, Donald (get acquainted meeting with prospect)				
3:30						
4:00						
4:30						
5:00						

Figure 13.3   Daily Planner, Filled In

shoes bought so as to "clear the decks" for the really important work. Yet, the reverse should occur, and only will occur with activities prioritization. The A activities must occur first and then the B. Those are the important activities and most aligned with the realization of goals. The rest of the non-goal-oriented activities can happen once the important ones are completed.

Let's factor in the concept of point of control. In meeting with Smith, who is an A priority because he will decide on taking action on our recommendations, we find that he has legitimate reasons for postponing his decision for a week. He promises to call back then once he's talked to his spouse, attorney, accountant, and so on. Do we let Smith have the point of control? Absolutely not, because he does not possess the same motivation as we. We want him to decide in our favor, and he will be potentially influenced by others and other factors and motivations. So we record Smith in our planner for later next week right after the day when he promised to call us. If he does not call as promised, we have the point of control and will reinitiate the conversation on our terms. Sounds obvious, right? Well, you may not be surprised to hear that many, if not most, people don't do this. They leave it to Smith and then are surprised to discover a month later when random memory kicks in that he hasn't called. Meanwhile a month has gone by, and much momentum is lost. In the same manner, if telephone calls are made, and folks are not available, do not leave the point of control with them to return the call. Indicate that a message was left on that day's planner sheet, and then mark it two days hence to follow up if they have not returned your message. This is all about your desired outcomes and the success of your business. You cannot afford to leave it to chance.

SUMMARY

1. The best, and maybe the only, way to reach your life's goals is through effective activities and time management.

2. Determine your goals in every aspect of your life: personal, family, spiritual, and career. But choose only one, or at most two, goals in each of those areas. You cannot do it all at once.

3. Do not be influenced by others, especially those who wish their agenda to be fulfilled at the expense of your goals.

4. Identify the actions that will take you to your goals.

5. Plan your day and week to allow for each activity required to reach your goals.

6. Plan your time *every day*. There are no throw away days or hours. There are lots of nonproductive time slots in everyone's schedule. For example, drive time could be used to hone business or personal skills with audio instruction or by keeping up with national, international, and business news that will help you make more informed business decisions.

7. Prioritize your activities using the A-B-C system. Do As first, Bs second, and Cs last or not at all.

8. Use time management tools. Write it down. Never trust your memory.

9. Retain and delegate points of control appropriately.

PEOPLE MANAGEMENT

Here too, you should not think in terms of "managing" people. Rather think in terms of structuring systems within which the good people you have recruited and nurtured can excel. See Chapter 4 on staffing and compensation. Peter Schutz, who turned around the Porsche motor company, presents an interesting view of this. He feels that effective managers work on the *systems* within which their people operate. Peter believes that the qualities of the well-hired associate or employee will prove their worth, and the manager's role is to engineer the runway, so to speak, and then let them "take off." Schutz feels that one should not work on people, but rather work on the systems and obstacles that enable or block people in reaching their full, innate potential. Before you dismiss this as unrealistic or new wave management, consider the advice of some fairly traditional sources on the subject.

First, Lee Iacocca is certainly not in the touchy-feely, new wave camp. He is a highly successful executive with a storied career at Ford, Chrysler, and with the national Statue of Liberty restoration project. He stated in his book, *Iacocca, An Autobiography,* that he began his career as a manager thinking of himself as an agent of change. He felt his successes with developing the hugely popular and profitable original Mustang automobile, his life-expanding Dale Carnegie training, and his experience to that point would enable him to change mediocre performers to ones that were superior. He felt he could accomplish this by sheer force of personality, will, and positive interaction. He confesses in his book that he was quickly humbled and came to realize that a manager, regardless of talent, cannot overcome 20, 30, or 40 years of prior life conditioning in his subordinates. Iacocca came to believe that the secret is hiring well, indoctrinating the new hire into the company's vision and mission, clearing the obstacles, and then letting him or her create and implement solutions and initiatives.

A second example comes from the U.S. Marine Corps and its fabled training of officers and noncommissioned officers. An uninitiated person might quickly think of the Marine Corps as a bastion of micromanagement where every Marine would be prevented from having an original thought. It is exactly the opposite. Every Marine, down to the newly minted private, is taught to think creatively. This is described in the book *Corps Business* written by David H. Freedman, an independent journalist. In that book, he recounts the Marine Corps maxim that no book of rules or battle plan can envision all that may happen in any exercise or combat engagement. Therefore, the Marine Corps places tremendous emphasis on and dedicating all of its resources to—you guessed it—the recruitment of good candidates, training, coordination of vision and culture, and the existence of good systems for operating. Individual initiative in the accomplishment of the mission's goals is highly valued.

The big payoff in adopting this philosophy by the business owner is that he or she can concentrate on areas that are most productive and profitable for the owner and for the business. In doing this, you will be an executive working *on* your business rather than a line manager working *in* your business. The following key actions are required:

- Hire the best people that you can find. This includes both sound hiring practices as well as appropriate skills and personality testing.

- Create the vision and the culture for your business. Become the chief cultural officer for your business. Be the best cheerleader for the positive attributes of your business within the company and outside too.

- Create systems to free yourself and your people from redundancy and mundane tasks. Allow them to create new solutions.

- Train your associates and employees in vision, culture, systems, but do not micromanage their activities.

- Hold people accountable for outcomes and give them the authority and autonomy to accomplish them.

TALK, TALK, TALK, AND TALK

Conversation is your best management tool. As the chief cultural officer of your company, you must always articulate your vision to your employees and strategic partners. Tom Peters, the internationally known writer, speaker, and business consultant, has counseled to frame one's vision message and deliver it consistently for six months. After that, he said, reframe it and deliver it for another six months, and continue telling it forever in one form or another. Only you can see where you wish your company to go, and it is your responsibility to transmit that vision to those on whom you will depend to implement it. Do not assume that they will intuit your vision from your actions. Although your actions should never be in conflict with your goals, they and your vision must be articulated at every opportunity.

We recently brought back a former employee who had taken a couple of years away to care for her family's needs. Although she thoroughly understood our operation, it proved worthwhile to discuss in detail where we are headed with our business. Her concluding comment was that the discussion helped her make her final decision to return to our employ. What we articulated was exciting to her, and she rejoined us with renewed energy. That may have happened anyway without the talk. But having that conversation helped assure that it occurred.

A scene from a story illustrates the point also. A 20-something young man did something that exhibited great character and personal values. The astonished, but proud, mother told him that she felt he had not been listening all of those years when she preached such character and values. The young man replied he too thought he had not been listening. But obviously the articulation of character and values—her vision for her son—had taken hold.

CREATING YOUR ORGANIZATION'S EMPLOYEE STRUCTURE

When you are starting your business, you may be the only employee out of economic necessity. But that should change quickly. You cannot do all of the duties required to run a business and attempting to do so will retard the growth of the business. It is not that you would be unwilling or think yourself too good for some duties. Rather, doing them will prevent you from accomplishing those activities and goals that may be crucial to the development of your company. Al Schnur, our consulting psychologist, put it well. He said he quickly realized when he bought his company and threw himself into building PCI Human Resource Consulting, Inc. that he should not be emptying the wastebaskets. The time used and the mentality he forced on himself by doing so were not conducive to building a world-class consulting and testing firm.

So as soon as you hire your first employee or associate, you must consider your management structure. You will need managers and workers. You cannot have everyone report to you. It can be emotionally satisfying for some people to be the go-to guy or gal. But you will quickly become the cork-in-the-bottle, and things will not flow as they should. Also, you will cut off the potential for creative ideas from your people because you will be making all of the decisions. So you must create a structure. How you structure your employees will depend on the organizational model you adopt as discussed earlier. If you need to, do not hesitate to contract for professional consulting to help you begin with a viable structural model that will facilitate your vision and help you to reach your business objectives faster. Consider two contrasting models for efficiency. The first model is typical of the startup entrepreneurship as it develops.

Owner			
Professional	**Professional**	**Professional**	**Professional**
Support	Support	Support	Support
Clerical/secretarial		Clerical/secretarial	

The problem with this structure is that every person on this personnel chart sees the owner as the key decision maker for every issue. So do the clients or customers. The owner is then pulled in many directions and can never fully focus on client development, visioning the growth of the company, and beneficial strategic partnerships. Consider the following as one possible alternative structural model.

Owner		
Supervising Professional		
Professional	Professional	Professional
Office Manager		
Clerical/secretarial support		

In this model, the owner has two direct reports, the supervising professional and the office manager. Those two individuals field all of the daily clutter, and the owner, while remaining in touch via direct reports, is free to do what should be done to grow the business. But often two obstacles get in the way. The first is the owner's ego. The owner built the business and is reluctant to give up authority and responsibility. Calm reflection would allow for an understanding that the owner's position is enhanced, not diminished, by this structure. The second obstacle is an unreasoned fear of increasing overhead. Profits are the result of an equation. And that is the following:

$$Revenues - Expense = Profits$$

If the owner is free to grow the business as a result of properly delegating duties, responsibility, and authority to two supervisors, greater revenues will be created. That is, after all, the result of growing the business. The small incremental increase in overhead representing the two managerial positions, with no increase in the number of employees, will pay dividends many times over as a result of the owner's increased productivity. That shift in structure requires a concomitant training of the two supervisors. It may not happen overnight, but it should not take all year either.

Our organizational structure may be illustrative of one that you might use as your business grows. Although we total only 24 people, that would be functionally unmanageable if all communication and activity strings came back to me (see Table 13.1).

Notice that I have three direct reports, and they have one or two direct reports and so on down the line. That allows for three benefits:

1. A manageable level of communication and responsibility is created for each manager so we all can concentrate on bringing and keeping business rather than having our days taken up with managerial details.

2. It allows for various levels of managers to grow with increased responsibility and for them to feel that they have a future within the company.

3. A forum is created for the creation of good ideas, and an avenue of communication exists to discuss and implement them. Not only are good ideas created, but also there is immediate buy-in because the idea was created and enhanced

Table 13.1

Managing Director—Owner					
Managing Director—Operations		**Managing Director—Portfolio Management**	**Managing Director—Sales and Marketing**	
Controller/HR Manager	Financial Consultant	Assistant Manager of Portfolio Management	Manager—Sales and Marketing	Financial Consultant
Administrative Supervisor	Financial Consultant	Portfolio Management Specialist	Sales and Marketing Assistant	Financial Consultant
3 Administrative Specialists	Financial Consultant	Portfolio Management Specialist	Intern	Financial Consultant
Receptionist/Appointment Scheduler		Portfolio Management Specialist		Contract Financial Consultant
		Financial Planning Analyst		Contract Financial Consultant

through the ranks. We also reward good ideas from support personnel with a $50 or $100 bonus.

The four managing directors meet monthly on primarily strategic and creative issues but also discuss multidepartmental tactical issues within the firm. An example of the latter would be the interaction of financial consultants and portfolio management specialists in the creation of client portfolio review materials. Contrast this structure to that of the typical small business. Everyone wants to get the boss's ear because no one else can make a decision. There is no glory in being the go-to guy or gal if it means that your business struggles or fails. And it very well may do that if you clog your communications and activity systems by making everyone come to you for answers, interpretations, and creative ideas. So begin with your first employee to create your vision of the eventual structure of your company that will best free you and everyone else to maximize your business's potential.

Making this a reality will not always be easy. Our industry is an example. Our strategic partner, Linsco/Private Ledger (LPL), is the securities-clearing back office for 3,300 small and larger independently owned offices. The thousands of conscientious and well-intentioned folks working within LPL are used to talking with the firm's owner when they have an administrative issue. Our receptionist is trained to cordially guide them to the appropriate person within our firm who can best deal with their question. Sounds so obvious? Yet, in many small businesses, that communications structure is never put in place, and the owner spends much of the day as the de facto receptionist guiding callers to the correct person in the organization. Some callers will do almost anything to get through to the owner, regardless of what they are initially told. That happens often for us with product providers. They wish us to consider their investment products for our clients and feel that, if they can just talk to the owner, they will have an in. In fact, they are far better served to talk to our portfolio management personnel than to me, and I advise them of that. The owner must be polite, but firm, in not allowing that sort of thing to happen. Once you do, it will always happen because the caller and your personnel will take the cue from you. Make sure that what you say and what you do coincide. That is what is meant by "culture."

As the business owner your most productive use of time includes the following:

- Creating the vision for the company
- Structuring it to operate most efficiently
- Recruiting and training personnel to fill the positions in the organization
- Creating new business by acquiring new clients and customers and by fashioning productive strategic alliances
- Fulfilling the role of chief cultural officer in creating the culture that will define and drive your company and then presenting that cohesive profile both within and without the company

Other appropriate personnel within the company should do everything else. Your goal as a sole practitioner in your start-up business is to grow it quickly so that you can hire the best talent to work within the structure that you have already created on paper. Your future is dependent on that. Until you have accomplished that, you have only traded one employer for another.

EVALUATE RESULTS BUT MANAGE ACTIVITIES

Proper delegation of responsibility and authority also involves the regular measuring of results by top management. For example, as chief executive officer (CEO), you will want to know your sales figures by department and by person even though your sales manager has the responsibility and authority of managing the sales force. That is as it should be. Further, the CEO also has the responsibility of visioning for the organization and, working with the sales manager, of helping to set and then approve specific sales revenue goals. The eventual revenues derived are compared against the original goals set for the period. The key to this process is that the results are *evaluated.* Inexperienced managers make the mistake of setting arbitrary sales revenue goals for departments and for individuals. Goals should be set based on objective criteria, and actual results evaluated based on the circumstances and the environment in which those revenues were created. This is not an argument for excusing sub par performance. Rather, it is a call for eyes wide open and in tune with reality management.

The danger in not setting goals and evaluating properly can be substantial. Inexperienced managers often set arbitrary revenue goals for others. They do this because they see others doing it—even some management books recommend this—and they do not have a better frame of reference. For example, a sales manager tells a transaction-oriented securities broker that he must produce $500,000 of revenue this year to stay on his career track. What if the markets do not accommodate that level of client portfolio activity? What if the best course of action is to keep clients in place and not turn over the portfolio? Creating revenues by fiat, regardless of circumstances, is in our opinion the cause of much malfeasance in U.S. business. Yes, goals must be set and results evaluated, but in a real time context.

The answer is to *evaluate results, but manage by activity.* In the preceding example, the sales manager is better advised to set activity goals for that broker that might include frequency of communication with clients, asking for referrals, and the number of educational seminars to be given during the year. In our experience, the correct amount of activity will inevitably lead to desired revenues over time. In fact, the revenue goals should be initially set based on an articulation of desired activity and then the calculation of average revenues provided by that activity. Your chances of keeping your people productive, making your clients feel well served, staying out of court, and achieving your desired level of sales revenues will be best achieved via activities management as opposed to the setting of arbitrary sales goals.

CREATING AND IMPLEMENTING YOUR BUSINESS'S STRATEGIC PLAN

There are three distinct, but connected, phases to your strategic planning:

1. Develop the plan.
2. Implement (make operational) the plan.
3. Communicate the plan both internally for employees and externally for all of your constituencies: clients, purveyors, and strategic partners.

Your strategic plan must be all of the following:

- Comprehensive
- Systematized
- Formalized

If not, it is simply conversation. And once implemented, *the results must be measured against objective and predetermined criteria.* Otherwise, how will you know if you have been successful in moving to your goals? The next section on determining what customers or clients you want will illustrate our company's folly in not measuring and evaluating client revenues and profits based on preestablished criteria.

A good book on the subject is Paul R. Niven's *Balanced Scorecard.* The concept of the balanced scorecard has been proclaimed one of the 75 most influential business ideas of the 20th century and is described as the method by which an organization may develop performance measures in four interrelated perspectives: financial, customer, internal processes, and employee learning and growth. According to Niven, the system is meant to help create performance measures that drive the execution of your strategy and provide the tools necessary to make the scorecard the cornerstone of your management process.

Bernie Wetzel, PhD, and Rick Alfera, CPA, located here in Pittsburgh have developed a personal service practice to help businesses implement the balanced scorecard. The originators of the concept were Robert S. Kaplan and David P. Norton who first published in the Harvard Business Review in January/February 1992. Their research indicates that only 5% of the workforce understands their company's strategy, only 25% of managers have incentives linked to strategy, 60% of organizations don't link budgets to strategy, and 85% of executive teams spend less than one hour per month discussing strategy.

That sounds to me a lot like making it up as they go, and certainly denotes the absence of coherent and coordinated goal attainment. So, regardless of the system you use, be it balanced scorecard or another, you have a mandate to tie your organization's activities to your vision and strategy for your business.

APPRECIATE AND VALIDATE OR THE DUCK SAUCE FACTOR

We must remember, and sometimes be reminded, to take time to appreciate those who work with and assist us along the road to effective management. Dale Carnegie taught that the greatest need of people is to be appreciated and valued. A personal anecdote may illustrate. About a dozen years ago, the author was asked to chair a committee for an organization that, because of its nature, was made up totally of women. Being a devotee of "the pugil stick effect," the author would acknowledge every successfully completed project with a quick "Okay, that's done, now we'll get on to the next project." The second time that happened, the women called a halt and declared that they wanted to stop, validate, and process the victory before moving on. They correctly explained that they deserved such acclamation for their efforts. After some fun bantering and conversation, I readily agreed, and we pledged to do so every time it was indicated in the future. But as old habits die hard, I would inevitably forget to stop and appreciate our successful efforts and allow time to validate. It had been our practice to meet over a lunch of take-out Chinese food at the organization's headquarters building. So, every time I forgot to stop to validate, a dozen female committee members pelted me with packets of duck sauce. It was a painless and fun way for me to remember to acknowledge this basic human need.

We all are advised to take the time to appreciate and validate the work of our employees. And where possible, it should be acknowledged in a specific manner. Simply saying, "You all did a good job on the project" is not nearly as meaningful as saying that along with mention of specific actions and results attained because of group effort. So "good job" should be coupled with something like "I especially like the way you pulled together and brought the project in under budget and two weeks ahead of schedule."

We will turn now from managing your personnel to managing your client acquisition and servicing for maximum growth and profitability.

WHICH CLIENTS OR CUSTOMERS DO YOU WANT?

When you are working with the pugil stick effect and whaling away gathering all the customers that you can, you are still well advised to have created a model for fitting them into an efficient customer management system. Some of you at the onset may decide to restrict your clients or customers by predetermined criteria. This could be by asset size, income, profession, geography, or any other such factors. Usually this is done for either or both of two reasons:

1. The service provider offers a specialized type of service or expertise and does not want to provide other services. An example might be a labor relations attorney or periodontist.

2. The service provider determines in advance the level of compensation he or she wishes to derive from any one client or business engagement and is not willing to accept lesser paying clients or customers.

Neither reason is wrong. That may be exactly how you wish to structure your business or practice, and your growth will be managed solely along the lines specified. But there can be a case made that this limits future growth as those who are not suitable clients or customers now may find different representation or service elsewhere, and the original discriminating provider will never have a chance to regain that lost business after the client grows in stature. We are not making a point here that either posture is correct or incorrect. But there may be a way to define your business's growth without becoming clogged with customers who do not meet your ideal characteristics today, yet still maintain a bridge to those customers who will grow in the future. Most new business owners will start off by not discriminating in accepting new clients or customers, so this section will be meaningful to most entrepreneurs.

The idea that certain types or levels of clients should not be accepted, or that they should be periodically purged to "upgrade" your client or customer base is a popular one in many industries. There are two pitfalls, we believe, with this thinking:

1. As previously referenced, some clients or customers will grow. Some will grow faster than others, and some will never grow. But as a group, your smaller or currently less desirable clients will evolve. To give them away or to keep them warehoused, so to speak, without proper servicing will prove detrimental to your future business growth. For a financial advisor, for example, to eschew the new physician just out of residency will probably eliminate the chance of that person becoming a top client in the years and decades to come. And if you are not thinking long term in your new business and are focusing just on today's business, you may want to go back to Chapter One and rethink your reasons for being in business. Building with a long-term future in mind is a chief reason people go into business for themselves. It should not be for today's highest dollar of income. More than 20 years ago, we gained a client who managed a local office for a national company. He was representative of many of the clients we sought then and now. He certainly was a hard working, smart, and nice person. We did not place arbitrary criteria on the acquiring of clients then or now. Today, without violating confidentiality, we can

categorize him as having investment assets that anyone would envy. (See the following paragraphs for the remainder of his story.) We could site many other stories just like his of young physicians and dentists who grew their practices over the years and middle managers who stayed mid-level management, but retired with or inherited significant assets that needed managing.

2. Satisfied clients, of any level of income, assets, or sophistication, are still your best source of referrals. They will refer you to their business associates, the other generations of their family, and even to other professionals or service providers. You may spend considerable amounts and significant personal time with advertising, public relations, and networking to gain new clients. Why not service well the clients you do have—at all levels—so as to have, in effect, walking billboards proclaiming your capabilities?

Now we'll return to the previous story of the local office manager. In the more than 20 years since he became a client, he has become one of our most prolific referral sources, encouraging coworkers and others to seek our advice. Early on, he introduced us to his CPA who also became a client and is a significant source of referrals to his other clients. Today, we have taken over the role of providing investment services to all of the clients of his accounting firm. The original client's daughter became an intern with us during college and is now a valued employee working in our portfolio management department. How much we would have missed had we followed the advice of some pundits who counseled arbitrary and shortsighted restrictions on the clients we accept!

MANAGING YOUR CLIENTS AND CUSTOMERS

Much like with time management, client management becomes a matter of correct allocation of resources. The author spent many years believing that every client deserved the *same* quality level of servicing. Thanks to the insight of one of our vice presidents, Christine Robinette, the author was convinced that every client deserves the *correct* level of servicing. Correct level is not synonymous with same level. Until that revelation was put into practice in our business, we were allocating the same level of regular client contact, administrative support, and firm resources to every client household. The result was that we were, in many cases, forcing servicing on clients who did not wish that level of contact. With the benefit of hindsight, we realize that we were filling the role of parent dispensing medication saying, in effect, "Take this. It's good for you!" Well, it was not adding anything and certainly was causing us to add more personnel to provide that level of support as we grew our number of clients. Be aware that these practices and results come about without being readily apparent and with the purest of intentions. But the diminished productivity and unnecessary attendant cost are harmful to the business nonetheless. Long-held, cherished beliefs would have never been changed without a corporate structure of openness to the creativity and fresh thinking of associates. The result? We did not in any way diminish the service provided to differing tiers of clients. Instead, we adjusted it up or down to a level that was appropriate to their respective needs and we freed up personnel and resources to be more effectively used within the company.

It Is as Easy as A-B-C and the 80/20 Rule is Alive and Well

You should create a client/customer structure for accepting new accounts into your business that immediately places them into the correct tier for servicing. Like time management, it should be as simple as A-B-C. Or, if you prefer, use Platinum, Gold, and Silver. You may even have a Bronze category. Here is how it may be differentiated:

A = The ideal level of client or customer that you wish to serve.

A+ = An A level client who is also in a position to influence referrals to you. This might be an A-level professional, such as a lawyer or accountant, who regularly sees the types of client that you want to meet. If you are starting a physical therapy practice, your A+ client would likely be an orthopedist or general practice medical doctor. Remember that every client can refer others to you. But the ones who have the greatest opportunity by profession or sphere of influence should have the + sign affixed to their designation.

B = This is the next level down in your criteria differentiation. It may be denominated by assets, income level, geography, or whatever. This is the client that is immediately productive for you, but just not as much so as an A-level one. The + sign becomes affixed here for referral opportunities also.

C = This would be everyone else. Here you must decide if you will accept C-level clients or customers. Our business model does accept them for the two reasons listed earlier. But we must be vigilant to service them correctly so as to not clog our system with clients who we are improperly overservicing.

It is important to realize that you will not give lesser service to your B and C level clients. You will give them service at a level appropriate to their needs. As their needs evolve in accordance with your criteria differentiation, so too will your service criteria evolve to meet that change. You may, for example, meet four times a year with an A-level client because he or she has needs and issues that indicate that frequency. By contrast, you may meet with a B-level client twice a year and a C once per year. Consider that previously we met with A, B, and C clients four times a year if we could force the C client to come in that often. So, an A, a B, and a C consumed 12 meetings per year. By changing the service standards to that described previously, we converted 12 annual meetings to 7. The freed up five meetings allowed room for another A client and another C client without adding servicing personnel. This is far different from the typical approach that service providers usually employ. Most have no service standards and react to everything anytime. So the squeaky-wheel clients or customers get the majority of the available time and attention, and the quieter clients with more potential get shortchanged on service and may drift away. This is why we refer to this as *managing* the business rather than simply working in it.

Let us look briefly at how this appears in the aggregate using our business's numbers at the time that Christine Robinette conceptualized and evaluated the problem. The following is what she found with our client base.

Client Category	% of Total Clients	Cumulative % of Total Clients	% of Total Revenues	Cumulative % of Total Clients
A	1.1	1.1	15.9	15.9
B	10.6	11.7	44.0	59.9
C	14.4	26.1	21.1	81.0
D	14.9	41.0	10.1	91.1
E	59.0	100.0	8.9	100.0
Totals	100.0		100.0	

It was very illuminating to find that our A and B level clients, our most desirable clients, represented only 11.7 percent of our total clients. Yet they provided 59.9 percent of our revenues. When we included our C clients, whom we also wish to service and retain, the total came to 26.1 percent of our clients who furnished 81 percent of our revenues. Although that disparity between percent of clients and percent of revenues was stark, it still seemed reasonable when one considers Peretto's Rule as it applies to business. Peretto stated that 80 percent of results come from 20 percent of activities. In our case, it was 81 percent of results as defined by revenues coming from 26 percent of our clients.

But the real shock was finding that we had 73.9 percent of our clients in the undesirable D and E categories, and they were furnishing only 19 percent of our revenue! Now before you conclude that we are all idiots at our company, consider that our firm is considered to be one of the more advanced, astute, and successful in our line of business. So we were progressing very well, although it turned out to be, if you will, rowing upstream using only one paddle.

Consider the amount of servicing and time invested in—forced on—those small clients. The solution was not to give away that 74 percent of our clients in the D and E categories. First, they had entrusted their financial goals and future to us. Second, the potential for referrals remained as described earlier. We had added personnel and systems to accommodate a level of client household servicing that was losing money in the lower tiers but profitable in total. So, the revenue from our larger clients was subsidizing the cost of servicing the smallest clients.

We had to engineer the correct service standards for the various tiers of clients. The way in which we did that may be helpful to examine, as it can be transferable to other businesses:

- The A level clients retained the four times yearly review meetings because their more demanding and sophisticated financial circumstances could benefit from that level of interaction. We even raised their level of service by adding monthly telephone call reviews of the portfolios.

- B level clients went to twice a year review meetings, and most were relieved to be rid of the other two meetings that we had tried to force on them. Their situations are well served with two in-person meetings supplemented with as-needed telephone calls.

- C level clients are now reviewed once per year, which is the correct level of face-to-face meeting time required for a more modest and less sophisticated account.

- D and E level clients were not given away. They were retained and are now much better served in a more automated system of portfolio management created by our strategic partner, LPL. They are serviced with an upgraded quarterly reporting system and a once yearly telephone call portfolio review.

Finally, the electronic and hard copy mail communication with every level of client was enhanced. Our portfolio management department transmits a summary of action and thought to every client monthly. This happens via batch e-mails sent economically by the Karol Company, an e-mailing service provider here in Pittsburgh, and by hard copy of the same letter to those clients who do not regularly use the Internet. All clients feel more connected, and it frees the financial consultant from having to make redundant phone calls.

The effort paid off. We freed up personnel time and were able to reduce staff mostly through attrition. We did not need to replace departing people given a more efficient servicing system. Also, the clients are benefited, as we would have had to raise our investment management fees had we continued on the same escalating servicing cost curve. Now new clients are properly fitted into their servicing tier, and we can handle many more clients at all levels without a diminishment in our ability to service them properly.

Also, as part of this value-engineering project, we discovered another productivity-enhancing opportunity. We had employed two distinct, but similar investment management systems. We found that our clients being managed under one system were not performing as well as those using the other. Over intermediate lengths of time, the investment performance was similar in the two systems. But in shorter time periods, and especially during market downturns, one system appreciably outperformed the other. One system is termed "nondiscretionary," which means we must call each client prior to enacting changes to their portfolio. The other is "discretionary," and we can make changes in the portfolios and advise the clients later. The nondiscretionary system entailed delays as we tracked down clients, and they thought over the recommended switches. Sometimes they just couldn't bring themselves to act. We believe that this time delay and sometime inaction contributed to the difference in portfolio performance, so that we changed all nondiscretionary accounts to discretionary. It entailed a fair amount of time and effort on our part to discuss and convince clients of the need to and benefits of changing, but change they did. The subsequent results bear out the benefits. The clients are in line for better results than under the old cumbersome manual system of portfolio management. Our personnel are working more productively and appropriately for each client. And although it was not an objective of the exercise, we reduced personnel by 14 percent, mostly through attrition, and our revenues went up 11 percent the following year.

It is important to understand that true service was not reduced through this entire exercise. Rather a cumbersome set of service standards was revised. We were expending energy and considerable personnel time trying to make clients submit to our well-intentioned, but misguided service standards. When we right-sized our level of service for each client household, the caliber of actual service performed went up in terms of functionality for the clients and for us. And by eliminating a less productive investment system, performance and client satisfaction went up. Good business management pays off for everyone.

TREATING CLIENTS AS PEOPLE

Creating efficient systems for managing your clients should serve the purpose of creating time to interact more meaningfully with them. Systems, standardization, and automation are meant to allow us to focus on our highest and best uses of talent and time. John Naisbitt in his landmark 1985 book, *Megatrends,* spoke to that point. He counseled that as we employ higher tech systems in our operations, we must correspondingly raise our level of client "touch." He coined the memorable phrase of "high tech/high touch" and named his subsequent 1999 book with that title. The intent of systemization and efficiency is certainly to *save* money, but much more importantly it is to *make* more money. And you do this by becoming closer as a result, not more distant from your clients and customers. Jack Mitchell has written a book entitled, *Hug Your Customers,* and it brims with ideas on creating customers for life. It all comes down to the concept of treating people the way you wish you were treated in every business transaction. We bought copies for all of our people and now refer to good client servicing ideas as "hugs."

Systematize for greater efficiency and then use the personnel time saved from manual processes to better connect to your clients and customers.

MANAGING DURING TOUGH TIMES

The entrepreneur is naturally an optimist and often a master of the pugil stick effect in terms of determination. This serves business owners well in overcoming the daily obstacles placed in their path. However, sometimes this optimistic, hard-charging mentality clouds judgment. This can be especially hazardous during business downturns. No one can be clairvoyant and know the evolution of current market cycles. But once a downturn is clearly identified, the business owner has an obligation to scrutinize the entire operation for efficiency. This should be an ongoing exercise in good times and in bad, but it can determine survival during the tough times. Some of the areas for special attention are illustrated by questions in the following paragraphs.

Are all personnel seeing the vision and contributing to the common effort? This is not about personalities, although a personality that is discordant with your culture often signifies counterproductive activity by that employee. Tough times require that all associates and employees strive on behalf of the business's health and continued survival, and toward improvement of market share at the expense of less efficient competitors. Take the opportunity and the mandate of a downturn to jettison those who you probably should have sent on to other pastures even during the good times but were lulled into keeping by prosperity. No one wants to play God with the life and livelihood of another. But to retain a draining influence within your organization risks the livelihoods of everyone else during business downturns. And your other employees know who those people are and are often much more realistic than you about what must be done. They will understand your actions.

Are there any company initiatives that are utilizing an unfair share of resources vs. the current or prospective revenues? This can be especially hard if the initiative was your idea, and you really felt it had potential. Keeping nonproductive initiatives that drain resources from your business is the same as keeping a nonproductive employee. You have an obligation to yourself, your family, your employees, and their families to make the best decisions that you can, regardless of how the initiative came about, whose idea it was, or how much money you had sunk into it before discontinuing it.

Are you being offered the best pricing for equipment, supplies, and services? This does not conflict with the goal of maintaining relationships. But every relationship has to be mutually beneficial. During the economic downturn of 2000–2002, we found that we could save considerable money by getting competitive quotes for what we buy. As a result, our phone service costs were cut substantially. Our supplies were also bought more cheaply from the very same supplier we had been using. They had not been taking advantage of us, as it wasn't their obligation to shop on our behalf. But once we did, they were more than willing to meet competitive pricing. We had used the same printer for years even when the shop was sold to a new party. But when we shopped competitively, we found that the equipment being used by that printer was causing unnecessary labor expense that was being passed on to us. The shop owner had no choice but to pass it on or buy updated and more efficient equipment to compete. He did not upgrade equipment, and we switched printers for substantial cost savings. It cannot be your obligation to make up for the business decisions of others. Just give everyone a fair chance to compete. You will not want to jump around chasing pennies, as that will label you adversely in your business community. But fair and regular checking of pricing will help keep your business healthy.

If you successfully explore these areas, and you have done a proper job of categorizing clients, establishing appropriate service standards, and positioning your service and products for maximum client value and efficiency, you will navigate through the bad times. You might even gain market share from less efficient competitors.

This mindset of enhanced productivity is readily transferable among industries. A discussion with a physician a few years ago centered on the turmoil engendered in the medical services community by managed care and attempts at severe cost reduction. The discussion resulted in an article published in the *Pittsburgh Business Times* that bears directly on this subject and is reproduced in Figure 13.4.

"But by rediscovering the clients and focusing on what makes them pleased with our services, we captured market share. Automation and other productivity-enhancing systems allowed us to then be profitable within that market share."

That is a fitting summary of this section.

PITTSBURGH BUSINESS TIMES

JUNE 19, 1998 — OPINION

What the investment community can teach doctors

The plight of physicians in today's climate of medical care evokes sympathy and empathy.

My clients include medical doctors and hospital administrators, and I see every day how beleaguered health care providers are by both bureaucracy and the constant shifts in regulation.

The medical doctor and administrator strive to give patient care in the context of seeming chaos.

I also empathize, as the investment industry went through the same metamorphosis, although not with the fanfare or widespread dislocation to the general public as the medical establishment is encountering.

The evolution of that may be illustrative and helpful today.

On May 1, 1975 (still referred to as "May Day! May Day!"), our sources of revenue became unfixed by federal government fiat.

This is analogous to the airlines' pricing deregulation.

The result was that thousands of independent investment firms, over the next several years, were swallowed by large organizations, and many others simply retired along with their principals, who didn't want to do business in such a climate.

Is this starting to sound familiar?

Those large firms set the rules for the rest of the industry and the federal government and regulatory agencies set even more rules to try to make this cataclysmic event somewhat manageable.

The results included a drastic cut in revenue for all firms from previously fixed levels to the lowest the marketplace and the regulators could engineer.

We also had to endure the sharing of the slim remaining profits by the large Or-

Commentary

Robert Fragasso

wellian organizations which by then had swallowed us.

I began in the investment industry in 1972 with a small organization that didn't survive the May Day aftermath and, like most everyone else, worked afterward within that type of large, faceless corporate entity until two years ago when technology and industry evolution made independent status feasible.

What's the point of this analogous history lesson?

While we saw our revenues decline by two thirds over previously, we also were besieged on all sides from new competition, which still exists today in the form of bank investment departments, Internet investment trading, Charles Schwab and many others.

During this painful transition, personnel were cut, salaries frozen or cut and whole new ways of doing business had to be devised. Meanwhile, many of our industry's personnel stayed mired in the old mindset and were a detriment to those who wished to not only survive, but find the right formula to thrive in this brave new world.

We had to find ways to do it with better automation, greater efficiency, less staff and, most importantly, with much less revenue per case.

The solution was to rediscover the client!

We no longer could act like the 1950s-era car dealership that held the only access to the product the public wanted before the Japanese auto invasion.

And we could not afford the luxury of inflicting our frustrations over the changes imposed on us on the very client we were now trying to court.

It wasn't the clients' fault that they didn't understand the changing landscape any better than we did.

It was our job to navigate ourselves and the clients through this maze while adding value we never had to add before — all for less money.

Those of us who didn't see it that way went on to other lines of work.

That's true of both individuals and whole companies. It also happened just that way in the airlines, the auto industry, the mainframe computer industry and now the medical care industry.

But, by rediscovering the clients and focusing on what makes them pleased with our services, we captured market share.

Automation and other productivity-enhancing systems allowed us to then be profitable within that market share.

Those who stayed inwardly focused instead of client-focused lost out.

Somewhere in this chaos and seeming darkness is the right mind set and formula for renewal.

I don't presume to know what it is. But I suggest that good people in the medical industry will develop it, and they and their patients will eventually be better off for having found it.

MR. FRAGASSO is a certified financial planner and president of the Fragasso Group Inc., a Downtown-based registered investment advisory firm.

Figure 13.4   Example of Enhanced Productivity

CHAPTER FOURTEEN

YOUR EXIT STRATEGY

Y ou are not taking it with you. You will work hard to build and manage your business, and one of two things will happen:

1. You will sell your business or your professional practice to others.

2. Your family member beneficiaries will carry it on.

You cannot now know for certain which of the two will occur—or when. So you must organize your succession planning as though it could happen tomorrow, as it may. Life is what happens while we are making plans. Let's view the following moving parts of a succession strategy:

- Price
- Who
- How
- Collateral issues

PRICE

A recurring revenue business sells for more than a transactional revenue business. A fee-based investment management firm will sell for more than a brokerage firm that transacts for commissions. First, the revenues are more plannable with recurring fees than with a transaction that must be reinvented over and over. Second, the recurring revenue business is less dependent on the skills and personality—the very presence—of the owner.

Your challenge is to determine how to make your revenues recurring. How can you make your relationship with your clients or customers happen on a renewable contract basis rather than on the basis of the whims of every day transactions? That translates to a much better business sale price. A rule of thumb in the personal service business is that a transactional business sells for one times annual revenues. A recurring revenue business sells for more than two times annual revenues. That is reason enough, but recurring revenues make your business life easier along with your exit. In addition, this arrangement is often better for your customer or client as the potential conflict of revenues for each transaction is removed. Would you rather, for example, be serviced by an investment advisor who is compensated by an asset fee that motivates him or her to make your portfolio grow or someone who earns a commission for making transactions regardless of results? It is good for you and good for your customers to make revenues recurring and, ideally, tied to your performance on behalf of the customer in some way.

WHO WILL BUY OR RECEIVE YOUR BUSINESS?

You probably cannot know this now. So you will have to consider all the possibilities: selling to strangers, selling to employees, or passing the business on to children. How old are your children? You cannot determine what may interest them at any stage until they reach their mid- to late-20s, if then. As you make hiring and investment decisions in your business, do it as though you will sell it to others. That will keep your decisions on the highest business plane possible. If your children later enter your business or profession, they should have to work their way up and prove themselves the same as any nonfamily members. Making sound business decisions along the way to hire the best and invest wisely in your business will not prejudice, but will enhance, the opportunity to integrate your family members into the business in a fair and productive manner.

HOW TO RECEIVE PAYMENT FOR YOUR BUSINESS

No rules we could set down here could possibly be universally applicable. You might sell your business for stock in the acquiring company, or you may sell it for cash. You could be given a lump sum payment, or you may receive periodic payments for a fixed or indefinite period. You will need to seek the best legal, accounting, tax, and financial planning advice available at that time. The following are some general admonitions:

- Investigate thoroughly the background and financial resources of the buyer, be it an individual or corporation. Many sellers have rued the day they were dazzled by a tremendous offer only to see later the terms of sale violated, and their company shattered. Yes, you can reclaim the business, but it could be damaged beyond repair by then, or you may not be physically or emotionally disposed to return to active management, let alone a Herculean business-rebuilding project. Do not rely on your own capabilities to do the required research. Acquire the best professional help that you can and do not allow for steps to be skipped.

- Have your accounting firm evaluate the tax implications of the sale. Weigh the advantage of getting everything paid comfortably up front versus the potential tax savings of a staged payment.

- If family members are buying your business, either through a purchase price or via continued salary to you and your spouse, be sure that you have everything understood and in writing.

You justifiably trust your children, but things happen, and others can become involved. What if your grown child divorces? How does the business play into the property division? What if the child who bought the business predeceases you? Will the estate be able to sell the business in such a way that does not prejudice you or your deceased child's spouse and his or her children? It may not work the way you wish, so advance contingency planning is necessary.

- Financial reporting requirements to you in a staged payment sale or continued salary arrangement will be important. You know the business as you built it. Although you will not wish to interfere with new management, be it stranger or family, you should have an early warning system in place to spot looming financial problems before your sale becomes hopelessly derailed.

Beyond these general cautions and action steps, you have a self-preservation mandate to proceed cautiously in the sale of your business. A responsible buyer will appreciate your due diligence, and it will only underscore the value of the business that they are buying. Deliberateness in the sales process will scare off only the unqualified buyer. If your business is saleable, it will sell, and cautiousness will not impede that.

SPECIAL CONSIDERATIONS IN SELLING TO FAMILY MEMBERS

You may have grown children who are buying the business, and others who are not involved. This can present problems from two directions. First, the nonbuying children can be unfairly treated at inheritance time when the bulk of your estate's value is represented by the business. If there are offsetting personal assets, the estate can be equalized among the business-connected and nonbusiness children. If sufficient assets are not available for equalization, a fair apportionment can be accomplished with insurance contracts keyed to a buy-out of the business at death. Seek competent tax and legal advice, but do not neglect this important aspect of your business planning. By properly arranging your estate, you are mentally freed to enjoy living today without the nagging guilt associated with important tasks put off. And you will advance peace and friendly relations among your surviving family members.

RETIREMENT PLANNING

Many entrepreneurs feel that they will work until they die, so retirement planning is not a priority for them. Still others plan to build the business and sell it for a grand pay off. Health, the vagaries of business, and changing family circumstances can conspire to thwart those goals. Business owners are well advised to begin their own retirement plans as soon as cash flow allows. We did not say as soon as cash flow comfortably allows because there will always be many competing demands on available cash flow, which will range from new business equipment to personal possessions. Make retirement plan contributions a priority for you. That built-up value at retirement, or on earlier disability or need, could spell the difference between comfort and crisis. Many types of plans are available to enact for you individually and for your company and its employees. Talk to your accountant and financial planner now. You will be thankful later. And in the likely event that things go exactly as you plan, the retirement savings is yours in addition to the buy-out price for the business or the lifetime payment from your kids.

THE END OF THE RAINBOW

You went into business for yourself so you could build something of which you can be proud. And you wanted to do it your way. The money was a reward, but was not the primary reason. Like Mae West, we know that considering the difference between rich and poor, rich is better. In addition, you will have the satisfaction of knowing that you have provided an opportunity for your employees and associates, and even your customers or clients, to raise their families and live a comfortable life because you created your business. Take great pride in that accomplishment. Maybe you were charitably inclined, and the success of your business allowed for improvements at the hospital, counseling for young families, the housing of homeless animals, or the healing of life's emotionally injured.

This happened because you had the will and the determination to create and nurture a business that succeeded. Those great benefits may not have accrued if you had stayed toiling at your old position. Now enjoy the fruits of your labor.

As you consider going into business for yourself, consider all of this as the outcome of your vision. For what are you waiting? The ancient question asks, "If not now, when?" Life usually rewards action and penalizes inaction. Give careful thought, make your plans, and then work your plans. Enjoy the journey and the destination—because it is yours to create.

APPENDIX A

READING LIST

This list is meant to provide supplemental assistance to you as you formulate your plans for your own personal service business. It is not necessary to read these books prior to beginning, and to do so will only delay your forward movement. Instead, please use them for additional ideas and to keep you positively energized as you go through your new business adventure.

The 5 Dysfunctions of a Team, Patrick Lencioni, Jossey-Bass.
> This book is a must-read for the effective melding of your team.

Advertising for Dummies, Gary R. Dahl, Hungry Minds, Inc.
> It is a basic but complete primer.

Aerobics Program for Total Well-Being: Exercise, Diet, and Emotional Balance, Kenneth Cooper, MD, Bantam Doubleday Dell Publishing Group.
> This is the update of Dr. Cooper's landmark book broadened to total fitness and includes his groundbreaking work in aerobics that was first published in the early 1970s. What profits a man or woman to gain the whole world and lose his or her health in the process? Plus, you work better when physically and emotionally

fit.

The Art of War, Sun Tzu, Shambhala Publications, Inc.

Much has been made of the use of these principles in business as in war. You do not have to be at "war" to fully use these timeless axioms.

Balanced Scorecard, Paul R. Niven, John Wiley & Sons, Inc.

Here is real world advice on developing a winning performance management system.

Bang! Getting Your Message Heard in a Crowded World, Linda Kaplan Thaler and Robin Koval, Currency.

This book examines advertising creativity based on knowing your market. Written by the creators of many of the most successful ads of our time.

Corps Business, David H. Freedman, HarperBusiness.

This is an absolute must-read written by an experienced journalist. It is based on the time-tested team building and management principles of the U.S. Marine Corps that have been forged on the anvil of life and death experience. Every principle is related to its potential use in business.

Dress for Success, John T. Molloy, Peter H. WydenPublishing.

This is different from other successful dressing books because it is based on extensive empirical testing on what makes people relate to us based on our choice of clothing. Although the book is dated, the concept of dressing based on desired results and not trendy fashion endures.

The Driving Force, Peter W. Schutz, Entrepreneur Press.

Here is a truly revolutionary concept by the executive who reversed Porsche's fortunes for the better. We all feel that we will be successful managers if we could just learn to manage people better. Schutz counters that the best managers engineer productive systems within which good people can operate. The business manager then recruits the best, articulates vision, and clears their path to work. It is an interesting concept that will take the reader beyond personality-based leadership.

The E-Myth Revisited. Why Most Small Businesses Don't Work and What to Do about It, Michael Gerber, HarperBusiness.

This is the book that will make you understand why and how you should be working *on* your business and not simply *in* it.

How to Sell Anything to Everyone, Joe Girard, Warner Books.

This is the saga of Joe Girard who made himself the top auto and truck salesman in the nation by mastering the pugil stick principle. But he did not become truly successful until he learned the value of building a team, delegating, and focusing only on his highest and best uses.

How to Win Customers and Keep Them for Life, Michael LeBoeuf, PhD, Berkley Books.

Here is an excellent how-to manual in creating a customer-centric organization.

How to Win Friends and Influence People, Dale Carnegie, Simon & Schuster.

This book is the classic. Reading this is the fastest way to learn how to relate to what other people truly want. This book embodies the secret to building a successful personal service business.

Hug Your Customers, Jack Mitchell, Hyperion.

Here is a terrific collection of examples of customer servicing and a wonderful small business success story. In a world of mass merchandised clothing, Mitchell and his family have built a business based on "hugging" their customers with world-class service.

Iacocca, an Autobiography, Lee Iacocca, Bantam Books.

This book describes management principles and insights from a master gained over a storied career.

The Leadership Secrets of Colin Powell, Oren Harari, McGraw-Hill.

Here is a book about character, values-based leadership, and teamwork

Marketing for Dummies, Alexander Hiam, IDG Books Worldwide, Inc.

This book is another good primer to help you understand the marketing of your business.

Megatrends, John Naisbitt, Warner Books.

In 1985, Naisbitt foresaw the technological revolution's permeation of our lives. And he sounded the warning to retain a commensurate "high touch" with the burgeoning "high tech" components of business and service. It remains as thought provoking today as when it was first written.

The Millionaire Next Door, Thomas J. Stanley, PhD, and William D. Danko, PhD, Longstreet Press.

This book will help you understand your marketplace and your own success patterns.

Mirror, Mirror on the Wall, Am I the Most Valued of Them All? The Ultimate Element of Differentiation is You, Leo Pusateri, Financial Entrepreneur Publishing.

A blueprint for creating and implementing your personal service company's value statement, this will be used in every aspect of your company and in your communication with clients and prospects.

National Compensation Survey, U.S. Department of Labor, Bureau of Labor Statistics, www.bls.gov.

Self-Employed Ownership Rates in the United States: 1979–2003, Robert W. Fairlie, www.sba.gov.

Think and Grow Rich, Napoleon Hill, Fawcett Crest.

Here is the masterful classic with insights based on the author's interviews with many of the founding giants of American business. It will guide you to a way of thinking that removes the clutter and focuses on objectives.

Unlimited Referrals, Bill Cates, Thunder Hill Press.

This is one of the best books on gaining referrals, well grounded in common sense and good taste.

Working Smart. How to Accomplish More in Half the Time, Michael LeBoeuf, PhD, McGraw-Hill.

The title does say it all. This is not simply a book of time saving ideas. It is a total mindset and—well worth your time.

APPENDIX B

THE
FRAGASSO GROUP, INC.

A REGISTERED INVESTMENT ADVISOR SINCE 1972 | WE GUIDE...YOU DECIDE®

Koppers Building, Suite 300, 436 Seventh Avenue, Pittsburgh, PA 15219 • 412.227.3200 • 1.800.900.4492 • Fax: 412.227.3210

Email: fgi@fragassogroup.com • www.fragassogroup.com

First Quarter 2005

Financial Success in the 21st Century

Are things different now? Do we need to think differently than in the past when defining financial success? Does corporate downsizing, shipping jobs offshore, technological innovation and the speed of change mean that we must seek new and different answers to our financial success and security questions? I pondered that recently as I viewed the almost century-old photos of the officers and members of Amen Corner— a 135-year-old Pittsburgh-based group comprised of members from a variety of professions. The people captured in that 1908 photograph must have wondered during the early part of the 20th century, much as we are now, about the rapid change enveloping them. Machines that had been developed as a result of the U.S. Civil War separated hundreds of thousands of people from their traditional means of livelihood in agriculture and in manufacturing. The United States had embarked on a military adventure against the Spanish in their territory of Cuba. This was promoted heavily by many and condemned by many others. Hotly contested presidential elections and the evolution of political parties and shifting platforms and constituencies proved very disconcerting to the people of the time. And, most ominous were the contentious wars being fought in distant lands by European powers, like

Bob Fragasso
President

the British and Germans in South Africa, over land, trade and economic advantage. People were even experiencing major cultural changes as young people moved away from home and their traditional values courtesy of the automobile. Even communication was thrown into turmoil. The telephone and radio redefined how people conversed and interacted. Business transactions sped to a then-dizzying level.

The comparisons to today are obvious. Productivity enhancing machines are still making some jobs irrelevant. World War II spawned inventions that have changed our lives just as dramatically as the Civil War inventions changed the lives of our ancestors. Substitute Iraq for Cuba and air travel for rail travel. Write the Middle East in for South Africa and view computers and the Internet in place of the telephone and radio. In fact, auto and highway transportation is still changing our geographical and emotional landscape. Change is inevitable. So, what remains constant? I believe it is human striving. We all want certain things for ourselves and for our loved ones. We seek financial security currently and certainly for our retirement years. We wish to provide our children and grandchildren with better opportunities than we had. That implies education at the college level and for specific and useable vocational skills. We wish to protect ourselves against unexpected adversity regarding health and safeguarding our possessions. And, finally, we wish our possessions to transition to people we love and to institutions that hold meaning for us. This has not changed and we believe it will not.

Success continues to be defined as it always has been. And the means of becoming successful have not changed either. Those means are categorized into three distinct action steps. First, define what you are trying to accomplish in your life – your life's goals. If you don't know where you are going, how will you get there? Second, marshal the resources that are available to you; those resources include assets, current income and future earning power. Third, create and implement a plan to get from where you are to where you wish to be. In doing so, you must use the time-tested principles of financial management— diversification, balance and asset allocation. Those are the principles honed on the anvil of long experience that have been historically proven to work. If applied properly, these principles can place us in the path of progress and offer financial advancement. By contrast, faddish, trendy, amateurish and overly-speculative techniques continue to work to our detriment as they have through past periods. This year, make your New Year's resolution one that builds on past success because the future is not much different than the past, it just appears so.

In keeping with our theme of defining success, we are initiating a profile of clients who have transitioned themselves along the road to success. Identification is a powerful instructive tool. As such, we begin our profiles with this issue and will continue in future newsletters as an attempt to assist our clients in progressing toward their life's goals.

We wish you a happy and prosperous 2005.

RETIREMENT PLANNING • WEALTH MANAGEMENT • EMPLOYER PLANS • COLLEGE EXPENSE PLANNING • INSURANCE • ESTATE PLANNING

Fee-Based Asset Management and Securities offered through Linsco/Private Ledger (LPL) Member NASD/SIPC

Best Bond Practices: Passive Ladder or Active Management?

There are two basic strategies for building a bond portfolio: a passive ladder strategy or an active management strategy.

Andrei Voicu, CFP®
Managing Director,
Portfolio
Management and
Financial Planning

Bond laddering involves investing equal amounts in bonds at staggered maturities. Active bond management, by contrast, attempts to adapt the portfolio through various market conditions.

Evaluating Risks and Rewards

Whatever the strategy, investors and their financial advisors should <u>always evaluate the total return of their bonds</u> (both the income, and principal appreciation or depreciation).

Investors should also recognize that there are three major inherent risks associated with any bond investment: *credit risk, interest rate risk* and *income reinvestment risk.*

As with many other things in life, only two out of these three risks can be controlled simultaneously.

<u>Passive bond ladder advocates state:</u> "I can just buy actual bonds and hold them to maturity, so I know exactly what I'm getting and don't have to worry about losing money. Plus I get the regular interest payments, and I don't have to pay the expense ratio charged by a fund."

<u>In reality:</u> Investors holding bonds until maturity tend to focus solely on income, at the expense of total return. Holding bonds until maturity gives the appearance of added safety, but risk management is mostly achieved by simply not looking at the existing risks. Ignoring the risks does not make them go away.

<u>Active bond managers state:</u> "Through the flexibility of investing in all sectors of the bond market, we are able to achieve better overall results than can be achieved by a laddered bond portfolio."

<u>In reality:</u> Forecasting interest rates and performing credit analysis are difficult tasks. Most active bond managers underperform their benchmarks. In addition,

high management expenses become an almost insurmountable obstacle to good performance in bonds. If expenses are too high, bond portfolios tend to either provide lackluster returns, take on too much risk, or both.

As with most all investments, there are pros and cons to both strategies. Whether passive laddering or active management makes the most sense depends on each individual's specific circumstances.

Bond Market's Current Environment

With the election behind us, some of the clouds of uncertainty floating over the markets have dissipated. Bond investors, however, continue to be plagued with indecision. Some suggest the economy is healthy, while others suggest that there are serious and dangerous structural problems within the economy. As a result, the bond market is teetering between expectations of inflation and deflation.

As your investment advisors, our job is to be neither optimistic nor pessimistic about the fortunes of the economy, but to be rational. Being rational helps us quantify the potential risks and rewards in order to prescribe the most prudent course of action for you.

Laddered Bonds

What a ladder bond portfolio *does* well:

1. It maintains a predictable principal value and provides attractive reinvestment of matured bonds in a rising-rates environment.
   - As bonds are held to maturity, they are always redeemed at par. As interest rates rise, lower-yielding bonds are replaced with higher-yielding issues. Discount bonds always appreciate to par.
2. It avoids the need for forecasting interest rates.
   - As maturities are staggered, maturing bonds in the short-term are replaced with new bonds that will mature in the long-term.
3. It can match cash flows generated by a portfolio with investors' liquidity needs.
   - The income generated is stable and predictable. Cash flows can be planned to service known liabilities.

What a ladder bond portfolio *does not* do well:

1. It does not maximize return potential.
   - There is a price to pay for predictability. Due to a lack of diversification, to avoid credit risk, laddered portfolios have to rely heavily on relatively low-yielding U.S. Treasury bonds or AAA-rated insured municipals.
2. It does not effectively provide for unexpected withdrawal needs.
   - Given its relatively rigid nature, a ladder portfolio is expensive to restructure following an unexpected portfolio cash outflow. Liquidating bonds prior to their maturity to satisfy unexpected investor's liquidity needs undermines the advantages of the ladder by re-introducing interest rate risk.
3. It does not allow for re-investment of income within the bond portfolio.
   - The income generated and not spent can only be reinvested at lower money market rates, as it is insufficient to allow for purchase of new individual bonds.
4. It foregoes capital appreciation and reinvests in lower-yielding securities during periods of declining rates.
   - As bonds are held to maturity and are redeemed at par, any previous capital appreciation is lost. Premium bonds will always depreciate to par.

Actively Managed Bonds

What an actively managed bond portfolio *does* well:

1. It offers instant diversification and unrestricted exposure to all sectors of the bond market.
   - Various sectors of the market offer attractive investment opportunities at various times. Having access to all sectors may increase potential return and/or decrease risk.
2. It offers reinvestment of dividends and capital gains.
   - Since a bond portfolio is a large pool of multiple investors' assets, the income generated is reinvested in the portfolio, allowing for compounded returns, which may result in higher future portfolio values.

3. It offers potential for incremental returns through higher flexibility.
   - The portfolio can be easily adjusted and rebalanced to reflect opportunities and risks in various sectors of bond markets at any given time.

What an actively managed bond portfolio *does not* do well:

1. It does not fully eliminate any of the three primary bond risks.
   - Risk management for interest rates, credit quality and reinvestment rests in the investment managers' hands. Successful risk management depends on the skill of the respective managers.
2. It cannot precisely match known liabilities with cash flows.
   - As there is no maturity schedule and bonds within the portfolios are constantly shifted, the timing of cash flows generated is less predictable.
3. It cannot be effectively designed and maintained without the commitment of performing the necessary due diligence and research.
   - The many variables of active bond strategies (tactical sector participation, management skill, expenses) need to be thoroughly researched prior to building a portfolio as well as on an ongoing basis.

What bond management structure is right for me?

While there is no absolute right or wrong answer, the investor's unique situation should dictate the right portfolio management structure. Depending on how you fit in as an investor within the scenarios listed below will influence what type of bond management strategy is right for you.

Some of the factors favoring a ladder approach are:

1. Investor has a well-defined, relatively stable income need. Investor uses bond allocation to provide income.
2. Investor puts a high priority on predictability of cash flows at the expense of additional potential return.
3. Investor has a large fixed-income portfolio that allows for building a ladder bond portfolio at a competitive cost.
4. Investor has sufficient reserve funds available and thus can avoid tapping ladder bond structure for emergency cash needs.

5. Investor does not have a strong conviction in the ability of available actively-managed options.

Some of the factors favoring an actively managed bond approach are:

1. Investor has no regularly scheduled portfolio withdrawals. Investor uses bond allocation to reduce portfolio volatility.
2. Investor needs or desires to reach an optimal risk/return tradeoff.
3. Investor's fixed income portfolio is not sufficient to permit building a ladder structure at a competitive cost.
4. Investor is concerned that any unforeseen future expenses may have to be met from bond portfolio.
5. Investor has a high level of confidence in active bond manager's ability to add value.

Of course, there is always the possibility to build a combined portfolio wherein laddered bonds act as a core, and actively-managed bonds add broad diversification. The Fragasso Group's financial consultants stand ready to discuss and recommend a suitable bond investing structure based on your individual circumstances.

The Benefits of Charitable Trusts

Many individuals fulfill their charitable inclinations with annual gifts to their favorite not-for-profit organizations. Although outright gifts of cash or securities are always appreciated, often, gifts made through a charitable trust can enhance the true value of the

Deborah Sales
CFP®, Managing
Director, Operations

donation for both the gifting individual and the receiving charity. Two of the most popular types of charitable trusts are the Charitable Remainder Trust and the Charitable Lead Trust.

A Charitable Remainder Trust (CRT) is an irrevocable trust that provides income to the donor and other named trust beneficiaries for the life of the trust. At the end of the trust term, the remaining assets are distributed to the charitable organizations named in the trust document. Upon creation, the donor irrevocably gifts assets to the trust, thereby removing those assets (and any future growth) from his/her estate. In return for the gift, the donor receives a tax deduction equal to the present value of the charitable gift which can be used for up to 6 years to offset as much as 50% of adjusted gross income (AGI) each year. In the end, the donor receives additional income and tax benefits beyond what is possible with annual giving. And the charities can mark on their books a future gift from this donor which may be larger than all expected annual gifts combined.

Conversely, a Charitable Lead Trust (CLT) is an irrevocable trust that provides income to a charitable organization for the life of the trust. At the end of the trust term, the remaining assets pass to the non-charitable beneficiaries named in the trust document (generally children or grandchildren of the donor). In this case, the donor receives a tax deduction for the present value of the charity's interest in the trust and benefits from a reduced transfer tax cost for the remaining assets that ultimately transfer to the non-charitable beneficiaries (family). So, again, the donor benefits from additional income and tax deductions beyond those available for the standard annual charitable gifts. And the charity continues to receive annual gifts via the trust.

The amount of income and principal distributed by the Charitable Remainder Trust and the Charitable Lead Trust depends on a variety of factors including the donor's age, the term of the trust and the expected growth rate of the assets within trust. The tax code also specifies certain guidelines that must be followed to fully benefit from the income tax and gift tax benefits associated with these trusts. Given the intricate nature of these trusts, it is important that you discuss the viability of a charitable trust as part of your overall financial and estate plan with your financial consultant at The Fragasso Group. Your financial consultant will evaluate your situation and charitable intents, advise you accordingly, and, if necessary, refer you to appropriate legal services.

3

Profile of Progress
A Client Story: Ed Leefer, D.C. and Ilene Cohen-Leefer, Esq.

By: Bob Fragasso, President

Ed Leefer and Ilene Cohen-Leefer and their children are representative both of our clients and of the people who help give our region its hard-working, family-oriented reputation. Ed is a chiropractor and Ilene is an attorney. They have two children: Jeremy, a 21-year-old who attended Penn State University and is currently interning with the Chicago Options Exchange Board and Eri, a senior at Upper St. Clair High School who will be attending Indiana University Bloomington. The course of their lives and their life today is representative of so many of our clients. For that reason, they are our inaugural client for this profile feature.

Ilene grew up in Stanton Heights. She received her law degree from The University of Pittsburgh in 1978 and worked as a litigator for the National Labor Relations Board for a decade before leaving to become a stay-at-home mom. In the late 1990s, she served as Executive Director of the Cambria/Somerset Labor Management Committee, an organization comprised of CEOs and their counterparts committed to improving labor management relations to enhance economic development. While raising her children, Ilene held leadership positions in varied non-profit organizations, including the Susan G. Komen Pittsburgh Race for the Cure. During this period of time, she became a certified group exercise instructor and personal trainer, both coordinating and teaching at local gyms and employee wellness centers, as well as providing personal back training for Ed's chiropractic patients. Currently, Ilene teaches pre-school at Temple Emanuel Nursery School in Mt. Lebanon where she has developed and is implementing a movement class for pre-school children.

Ed grew up in Munhall, the son of a veterinarian who maintained a career-long practice in the area. He attended West Virginia University studying for a degree in business. While there, he suffered from a stomach ulcer that was being properly treated medically, but still recurring. On a recommendation, Ed visited a chiropractor who evaluated a misaligned spine and corrected that condition through chiropractic therapy. During that process, the ulcer disappeared. Ed was convinced that chiropractic practice was his future. He enrolled in the Palmer College of Chiropractic and graduated in 1974. Ed spent his first year gaining experience working in the offices of others before borrowing money and opening his own practice in 1975. When he opened his doors, the immediate challenge was to make people aware of his profession and location, 5800 Brownsville Road in the Pleasant Hills section of Pittsburgh (the same location out of which he practices today). He immediately used some of that borrowed money to hold an open house with appropriate publicity and quickly signed up 63 new patients. Meeting Ed now, you would not be surprised at those results, as his kind and gentle manner immediately instills comfort and trust. A local newspaper once characterized Ed as practicing "in a way that allows him to get to know each and every person that seeks his care."

A personal example illustrates this. The author suffered a multiple break ankle injury in 1988. After six months of operations and non-weight-bearing casts, the author began

The Leefer Family: Jeremy, Eri, Ilene and Ed

exercise therapy. There seemed to be perpetually pulled back muscles that the author attributed to exercising. This was mentioned to Ed at a client review meeting and, typical of Ed, he did not suggest visiting him. He awaited the author's realization of that potential benefit. Up to then, the recommended solution by others was muscle relaxant medication, with all of the attendant side effects. At the first visit, Ed demonstrated with X-rays that the months of imbalanced movement on crutches had caused several vertebrae to turn and press on nerves. This was the source of the pain, not pulled muscles. After two months of chiropractic therapy, the vertebrae were returned to their proper position and the pain was gone – never to return. No medication and no surgery would be needed. Ed is fortunate to be able to make a comfortable living and help people in the process.

But, professional practice and life do not run a consistently smooth course despite hard work, good intentions and competency. In the early 1990s, Ed experienced what all of our medical profession clients have endured – the advent of managed care. While most agree with the need to control costs, the severity of the actions taken at the federal level and by individual health care insurance providers caused a cataclysmic shock to medical care providers. In Ed's case, people who sought care could not access it because most managed care plans offered financial incentives to "gatekeepers" to deny or severely restrict referrals to specialists. Managed care challenged Ed's practice but, he found ways to rebuild it and continue to offer superior patient care. Today, Ed participates in and provides care through all of Highmark Blue Cross/Blue Shield and all of Highmark's managed care plans as well as UPMC, Health America, Cigna, United Healthcare and Medicare.

What do Ed and Ilene care about today? They want the same things that you likely do. They want their children to have an education that allows them to actualize and to provide for their families some day. While Ed and Ilene never expect to retire, they wish to have the financial security that allows them the freedom to decide. Knowing that they have provided for each other and for their children allows them to proceed through life comfortably and happily. They were prudent through the years and we are pleased and proud to have provided them with the advice and guidance they sought from us. We feel this sense of gratitude about all of our clients and are proud to count Ed and Ilene among our friends.

4

Municipal Bond Basics

At first glance, a municipal bond may seem like a complex investment. In reality, it is little more than a loan. When a municipality issues a bond, it's asking you and other investors to lend it the funds it needs. In return, the municipality (the borrower) promises to pay you interest until the bond's maturity, when the loan is repaid.

The interest (the income you earn on your municipal bond investment) is free from federal, and in some cases, state and local taxes. In other words, you get to keep more money.

Michael Fertig
Managing Director,
Sales and Marketing

The attractive benefits of municipal bonds are also passed along to investors of municipal bond funds. Often called "muni funds," these investments are an affordable way for investors to earn federally tax-free income while enjoying the advantages of a professionally-managed portfolio.

All too often, purchasing individual municipal bonds can prove to be cost-prohibitive for individual investors as they typically require a $5,000 minimum investment. That may make it difficult to gain the adequate diversification necessary for a properly-balanced portfolio. But, by pooling investors' capital, a muni fund's management team can invest that money in a variety of municipal bonds and achieve a greater and more appropriate level of diversification than the average investor could achieve by simply investing on his or her own.

Initially, a municipal bond fund's yield might not seem as impressive as that of a taxable bond fund. However, for a clearer view, we must bring taxes into the equation. The yield on a taxable bond fund reflects income earned before taxes. But, because a municipal bond fund's interest income is tax exempt from federal taxes, we need to look at its tax equivalent yield.

Consider this example:

The table below shows how the money invested in a taxable bond fund must work harder to achieve the tax-free equivalent yield of a municipal bond fund. For example, for a couple filing a joint return in the 30% tax bracket, a seemingly modest 7% tax-free yield is actually comparable to a 10% yield on a taxable investment. Their money has to work much harder for ultimately the same take-home earnings.

Assuming a 30% tax bracket:

If Your Tax-Exempt Yield With A Muni Fund Is:	Then Your Equivalent Yield On A Taxable Investment Would Need To Be:
3.0%	4.29%
5.0%	7.14%
7.0%	10.00%

If you would like to determine the tax equivalent yield for yourself, follow this formula:

$$\frac{\text{TAX-FREE YIELD}}{[1-(\text{Your Tax Rate})]} = \text{Taxable Equivalent Yield}$$

If you would like to know if a municipal bond investment might be right for you, please call your financial consultant at The Fragasso Group. We would be happy to discuss the possibility for your situation.

RSVP COMMUNITY SERVICE VOLUNTEER OF THE YEAR

Sally and Bob at the luncheon

The Fragasso Group is once again proud to have sponsored the Retired and Senior Volunteer Program (RSVP) award for Community Service Volunteer of the Year. On October 12, Bob Fragasso presented the award to Sally Ford of Rosslyn Farms at a luncheon held at the Sheraton Station Square. Sally is the grandmother of nine and, at age 79, still finds the time and energy to exert a "positive influence on the lives of countless children by working with small groups as well as individual students."

The award nomination details Sally's contributions and characteristics: "Sally always listens and has positive and comforting comments for the children." However, the children are not the only beneficiaries of her devotion to Carnegie Elementary School. Her efforts are also very much appreciated by the entire staff.

At The Fragasso Group, we believe Sally has touched many young lives and her work has and will continue to make an impact on those children and our region simply because she cared enough to get involved and make a difference. We extend our tribute to Sally and all of her counterparts throughout our region who care enough to make that difference.

5

Ring in the New Year with Knowledge!

Dana Dagnal
Manager, Marketing
and Seminars

As we ring in another New Year, it is time once again to begin our educational financial planning seminar series. As many of you are already aware, the University of Pittsburgh is in the process of reconfiguring its lifetime learning courses. As a result, we are thrilled to announce our new relationship with another educational institution that contributes to our region: The Community College of Allegheny College (CCAC).

We will be utilizing four of the college's convenient suburban locations for our Winter and Spring 2005 seminars. The locations are as follows: Allegheny Campus on the North Side, North Campus in Wexford, Boyce Campus in Monroeville, and Bethel Park Center in Bethel Park. We are looking forward to a long-term relationship with CCAC.

As always, if there are people you feel may benefit from attending one of our seminars, please pass along the information below. We look forward to seeing you there!

Winter/Spring 2005 Seminar Schedule

Monroeville Campus	Allegheny Campus	Bethel Park Center	North Campus
MONDAYS	**TUESDAYS**	**WEDNESDAYS**	**THURSDAYS**
Personal Financial Planning Workshop February 28, March 7, 14 6:30 p.m.-9:30 p.m.	Women On Their Own February 15, 22, & March 1 6:00 p.m.-9:00 p.m.	Can You Afford To Retire? February 23, March 2, 9 6:30 p.m.-9:30 p.m.	Personal Financial Planning Workshop February 17, 24, & March 3 6:30 p.m.-9:30 p.m.
Can You Afford To Retire? March 21, 28 & April 4 6:30 p.m.-9:30 p.m.	Can You Afford To Retire? March 8, 15, 22 6:00 p.m.-9:00 p.m.	Personal Financial Planning Workshop March 16, 23, 30 6:30 p.m.-9:30 p.m.	Women On Their Own March 10, 17, 24 6:30 p.m.-9:30 p.m.
Women On Their Own April 11, 18, 25 6:30 p.m.-9:30 p.m.	Financial Security During Retirement March 29, April 5, 12 1:00 p.m.-4:00 p.m.	Financial Security During Retirement April 6, 13, 20 1:00 p.m.-4:00 p.m.	Can You Afford To Retire? March 31, April 7, 14 6:30 p.m.-9:30 p.m.
Financial Security During Retirement May 2, 9, 16 1:00 p.m.-4:00 p.m.	Personal Financial Planning Workshop April 19, 26 & May 3 6:00 p.m.-9:00 p.m.	Women On Their Own April 27, May 4, 11 6:30 p.m.-9:30 p.m.	Financial Security During Retirement April 21, 28 & May 5 1:00 p.m.-4:00 p.m.

For any questions you may have concerning the information in these articles, please call your financial consultant at The Fragasso Group or visit us at www.fragassogroup.com.

Our Commitment To YOU!

What is our Commitment to You?

Linsco/Private Ledger Corp. (LPL) and its family of affiliated companies are committed to maintaining the trust and confidence of our clients. As such, we want you to understand how we protect your privacy when we collect and use information about you, and the measures we take to safeguard that information.

Diana Schroeder
Administrative Manager

Keeping client information secure and private is a priority for us. The following describes our Privacy Policy. Please take a moment to review it and feel free to contact us with any questions. Thank you for the trust you have placed in us. We continue to work hard to earn that trust.

What types of non-public personal information do we collect about you?

In the course of providing services to you, we collect non-public personal information about you from the following sources:

- Information on account applications and other standard forms (i.e., name, address, social security number, assets, types and amounts of investments, transactions, and income)
- Information about your LPL transactions, our affiliates or others including those companies that work closely with us to provide you with diverse financial products and services (i.e., your account balance, payment history, parties to transactions, types and amounts of investments, transactions, and credit card usage)

- Information we receive from consumer reporting agencies (i.e., your credit worthiness and credit history)
- Information obtained when verifying the information you provide on applications or other forms (this may be obtained from your current or past employers, or from other institutions where you conduct financial transactions)

How do we protect the confidentiality and security of your non-public personal information?

Keeping your information secure is one of our most important responsibilities. Access to non-public personal information about you is restricted to those employees and agents who need to know that information in order to provide you with products or services. We maintain physical, electronic, and procedural safeguards that comply with federal standards to guard your non-public personal information.

Do we disclose to any non-affiliated third parties your non-public personal information?

We do not sell, share or disclose your non-public personal information to non-affiliated third-party marketing companies.

We may disclose all of the information we collect, as described above in the "What types of non-public personal information do we collect about you?" section to companies that perform marketing or other services on our behalf, or to other financial institutions with whom we have joint marketing agreements. All of these companies are contractually obligated to keep the information that we provide to them confidential and use the information only for the services required and as allowed by applicable law or regulation, and are not permitted to share or use the information for any other purpose.

We may also disclose non-public personal information about you under circumstances as permitted or required by law. These disclosures typically include information to process transactions on your behalf, to conduct our operations, to

follow your instructions as you authorize, or to protect the security of our financial records.

Do we disclose within our family of affiliated companies your non-public personal information?

In the course of providing services to you, we are permitted by law to share within our family of affiliated companies information about our transactions or experiences with you (such as account balance or payment history).

What is our policy relating to former customers?

If you decide to close your account(s) or become an inactive client, we will adhere to the privacy policies and practices as described in this notice.

We reserve the right to change this policy at any time and you will be notified if any changes occur. If you have any questions after reading this Privacy Policy, please write to:

> Privacy Management
> c/o Legal Department
> Linsco/Private Ledger Corp.
> One Beacon Street, 22nd Floor
> Boston, MA 02108-3106

This Privacy Policy applies to those who are current or former clients of the LPL family of affiliated companies in the United States. The LPL family of affiliated companies are Linsco/Private Ledger Corp., its subsidiaries and affiliates, including Independent Advisers Group Corporation, LPL Insurance Services, Inc., LPL Insurance Services of Colorado, Inc., Private Ledger Insurance Services of California, Inc., Private Ledger Insurance Services of Massachusetts, Inc., Private Ledger Insurance Services of Nevada, Inc., Private Ledger Insurance Services of New Mexico, Inc., Private Ledger Insurance Agency of Ohio, Inc., Private Ledger Insurance Services of Oklahoma Agency, Inc., PL Insurance Services of Texas, Inc., and Linsco/Private Ledger Corp. of Wyoming, Inc.

7

THE
**FRAGASSO
GROUP**, INC.
WE GUIDE...YOU DECIDE®

Koppers Building, Suite 300
436 Seventh Ave.
Pittsburgh, PA 15219

IRA Participants or Qualified Retirement Plan Participants Over Age 70 ½, and Owners of Beneficiary IRAs, This Is For You!!

This month, LINSCO/Private Ledger will be mailing to you directly a letter and form regarding your Required Minimum Distribution (RMD) for 2005. IRS regulations require us to notify you by January 31st of each year.

Please sign the form immediately and return to us at the below address:
The Fragasso Group
Koppers Bldg. Suite 300
436 7th Avenue
Pittsburgh, PA 15219

Do not use the LINSCO/Private Ledger envelope sent to you. Upon receipt at our office, your financial consultant will call you to discuss the actual processing of this form.

Look for it in your mailbox!

EMAIL UPDATE

If you are not currently receiving our monthly eNewsletter or other e-mail updates, please send your e-mail information to:

fgi@fragassogroup.com

200

An eNews Update to our Quarterly Newsletter

December 2004

In addition to keeping your portfolio well balanced, you must also be aware of the potential tax issues that exist anytime you decide to sell a security. You need to regularly re-evaluate your portfolio to ensure that your allocations and balances are still appropriate. In doing so, you may identify investments that have dropped in value and do not appear to be poised for a rebound. If you decide to sell in order to reinvest in another security with more potential, and have taxable gains from other investments, a tax-loss sale can work to your advantage. This is what the professionals at The Fragasso Group work to do on your behalf as part of our normal year-end tax planning process. Here is an example of how it can work:

By: Mike Fertig
Managing Director,
Sales and Marketing

STEP 1 Harvest the Tax Loss

An investor purchased $10,000 in ABC Stock Fund prior to December 31st in Year One. In December of Year Two the fund's value is $5,000, giving the investor a $5,000 long-term capital loss (LTCL).

NOTE: Tax-loss selling works only for funds held in taxable accounts and not those in retirement plans, such as IRA's and 401(k)'s.

STEP 2 Offset Capital Gains

The investor also owned XYZ Stock Fund, which distributed $1,000 in long-term capital gains (LTCG) in Year Two (a taxable capital gain can come from a variety of investments, including the sale of a stock, mutual fund or appreciated real estate).

NOTE: To calculate taxes, the investor applies all capital losses against capital gains, giving the investor a net capital loss of $4,000. Realized short-term capital losses must first be used to offset short-term capital gains, then long-term gains. Similarly, long-term losses must first offset long-term gains, then short-term gains.

STEP 3 Offset Ordinary Income

After first applying capital losses against capital gains, the investor may apply excess losses against up to $3,000 in ordinary income, including wages, dividends and interest.

STEP 4 Carry Losses Forward

The investor can now carry a net capital loss in excess of Year Two capital gains and $3,000 in ordinary income for an unlimited time until the loss is exhausted. Losses that are carried forward retain their long- or short-term

201

status and must first be used to offset similar gains in future years, then may be applied against ordinary income.

STEP 5 Reinvest

The investor now has to carefully decide what to do with the $5,000 from the sale of ABC Stock Fund from Step 1. Because most mutual funds declare capital gains distributions in the fourth quarter, the investor is at risk of buying a mutual fund that is poised to make a capital gains distribution. This is a taxable distribution even if reinvested and could erase the benefit of a tax-loss sale. Also, the IRS prohibits taking a loss if an investor purchases the same investment or a "substantially identical" investment in the period beginning 30 days before the date of the sale and ending 30 days after the sale. (For further information, please contact your Fragasso Group financial advisor or visit us at www.fragassogroup.com/directory.html.)

Bottom line: Investment Decisions and Tax Issues Go Hand in Hand

The decision to sell an investment that has dropped in value should not be made solely on the basis of tax implications. Before deciding to sell any investment at a loss, you should carefully consider the impact on your total portfolio. But once you've identified a holding you no longer believe is right for you, tax-related information can make the decision to sell easier.

The professionals at The Fragasso Group enlist this process when evaluating your portfolio for possible adjustments. Our experience, commitment and knowledge work collaboratively to ensure that you continue toward your financial life goals.

For more information or if you have any questions, please call 412-227-3200 or email me at michael_fertig@fragassogroup.com.

This article is for informational purposes only and not intended as tax advice. Consult your tax advisor to determine what is appropriate for your situation.
Past performance is no guarantee of future results.

If you have any comments, questions or suggestions concerning this electronic newsletter, please email us at fgi@fragassogroup.com.

Click here if you do not want to continue receiving The Fragasso Group eNews.

Visit Our Web site:
www.fragassogroup.com

A REGISTERED INVESTMENT ADVISOR
The Retirement Planning and Wealth Preservation Specialists Since 1972
Koppers Building, Suite 300, 436 Seventh Avenue, Pittsburgh, PA 15219-1818

Phone 412.227.3200, Fax 412.227.3210, Toll Free 1.800.900.4492
Fee-based asset management and securities offered through Linsco/Private Ledger (LPL)
Member NASD/SIPC

INDEX

ABOUT THE
AUTHOR

Robert Fragasso is the founder and president of The Fragasso Group, Inc., an investment management and financial planning firm located in Pittsburgh, Pennsylvania. He has 33 years experience in his field. But, until nine years ago, he housed his team within a large national organization. This guide to independence for the personal service provider is based on his 33 years of experience in creating a top-tier financial services firm within an extremely competitive, fragmented, and crowded industry. This guidebook contains the hard-won lessons he learned in breaking off his team into his own company. Fragasso feels that, by providing you with this guide based on his real life experiences, you too can build a business of your own in your chosen area of personal service. Be you attorney, accountant, architect, medical services provider, or management consultant, you can plan, create, and manage your own business successfully and capitalize on the strength of being smaller and flexible.

You can contact Bob at robert_fragasso@fragassogroup.com.